PLOUGHSHARES

Spring 1997 · Vol. 23, No. 1

GUEST EDITOR
Yusef Komunyakaa

EDITOR
Don Lee

POETRY EDITOR
David Daniel

ASSISTANT EDITOR
Susan Conley

ASSISTANT FICTION EDITOR
Maryanne O'Hara

FOUNDING EDITOR
DeWitt Henry

FOUNDING PUBLISHER
Peter O'Malley

PLOUGHSHARES, a journal of new writing, is guest-edited serially by prominent writers who explore different and personal visions, aesthetics, and literary circles. PLOUGHSHARES is published in April, August, and December at Emerson College, 100 Beacon Street, Boston, MA 02116-1596. Telephone: (617) 824-8753. Web address: http://www.emerson.edu/ploughshares/.

EDITORIAL ASSISTANTS: Jessica Olin, Dina Finz, and Tom Herd. POETRY READERS: Richard Morris, Caroline Kim, Renee Rooks, Michael Henry, R. J. Lavallee, Jessica Purdy, Brijit Brown, Tom Laughlin, Bethany Daniel, Charlotte Pence, Lori Novick, and Ellen Scharfenberg. FICTION READERS: Heidi Pitlor, Billie Lydia Porter, Leah Stewart, Monique Hamzé, Thomas McNeely, Craig Salters, Tammy Zambo, Emily Buol, Karen Wise, Michael Rainho, Ellen Tarlin, Jodee Stanley, John Rubins, Holly LeCraw Howe, David Rowell, and Kevin Supples.

SUBSCRIPTIONS (ISSN 0048-4474): $21 for one year (3 issues), $40 for two years (6 issues); $24 a year for institutions. Add $5 a year for international.

UPCOMING: Fall 1997, a fiction issue edited by Mary Gordon, will appear in August 1997. Winter 1997–98, a fiction and poetry issue edited by Howard Norman & Jane Shore, will appear in December 1997.

SUBMISSIONS: Reading period is from August 1 to March 31 (postmark dates). Manuscripts sent from April to July are returned unread. Please see page 227 for detailed submission policies.

Classroom-adoption, back-issue, and bulk orders may be placed directly through PLOUGHSHARES. Microfilms of back issues may be obtained from University Microfilms. PLOUGHSHARES is also available as CD-ROM and full-text products from EBSCO, H.W. Wilson, Information Access, and UMI. Indexed in M.L.A. Bibliography, American Humanities Index, Index of American Periodical Verse, Book Review Index. Self-index through Volume 6 available from the publisher; annual supplements appear in the fourth number of each subsequent volume. The views and opinions expressed in this journal are solely those of the authors. All rights for individual works revert to the authors upon publication.

PLOUGHSHARES receives additional support from the Lannan Foundation and the Massachusetts Cultural Council. Marketing initiatives are funded by the Lila Wallace–Reader's Digest Literary Publishers Marketing Development Program, administered by the Council of Literary Magazines and Presses.

Distributed by Bernhard DeBoer (Nutley, NJ), Fine Print Distributors (Austin, TX), Ingram Periodicals (La Vergne, TN), Koen Book Distributors (Moorestown, NJ), and L-S Distributors (S. San Francisco, CA).

Printed in the U.S.A. on recycled paper by Edwards Brothers.

© 1997 by Emerson College

CONTENTS

Spring 1997

Crossroads

The crossroads is a real place between imaginary places—
points of departure and arrival. It is also a place where negoti-
ations and deals are made with higher powers. In the West African
and Haitian traditions of Legba, it is a sanctified place of reflection
(mirrors are used in symbolic travel). The crossroads is a junction
between the individual and the world.

When I was asked to edit this issue of *Ploughshares*, I did not
have a thematic trope in mind. But halfway into the editing, after
the wonderful stories and poems had begun to accumulate, a
shaped presence began to jell within the collection. As if from
some unknown station, the characters and narrators began to
wander across varied psychological and emotional territories, and
the shape of the crossroads imprinted itself on this issue of
Ploughshares.

Maybe this overall feeling also arose from the energy of *The Sky
Is Crying: The History of Elmore James* pouring from the Sony
speakers. James's "Standing at the Crossroads" conjured up
Robert Johnson. Momentarily, as I sat in my Park Plaza apartment
in St. Louis, reading and rereading the stories and poems, I
glimpsed that legendary figure standing somewhere in the Missis-
sippi Delta night, clutching his guitar, ready to make a Faustian
deal with the devil. But, of course, it wasn't long before the Delta
night became a countryside road somewhere in Haiti.

From the cult of Legba, my mind turned to the essence of the
Cross. Since creative artists are indebted to the industry of sym-
bolism and numinosity (concerned with how the object is a map
for the internal terrain), at this juncture it became illuminating to
embrace C. G. Jung: "...the imagination liberates itself from the
concretism of the object and attempts to sketch the image of the
invisible as something which stands behind the phenomenon. I
am thinking here of the simplest basic form of the mandala, the
circle, the quadrant or, as the case may be, the cross." As with
most myths and legends, each is a composite of contradictions

and oppositions. Example: Constantine's dream of the cross was probably prompted by how the streets of Rome were patterned; Robert Johnson's deal with the devil probably occurred beneath a full moon somewhere in San Antonio, Texas.

In this sense, many of the stories and poems in this issue seem to exist in two or more places simultaneously, and a narrator or speaker is forced to negotiate multiple worlds. There is an accrued bravery here. It is this cultural dualism, this ability to be two places at once, to be a shape-changer, that strengthens the creative quest. Thus, this collection has a fractured design. There's a jagged persistence that documents and duplicates the awkward reality of our contemporary lives and imaginations.

Many of us are still reeling from the death of Larry Levis. And since this issue of *Ploughshares* encompasses numerous paths and diversions, it seems natural to dedicate it to the memory of this American poet who created bridges through his poetry. Throughout his several books Larry was not afraid to invite voices from all communities into his vision. His was a poetry of inclusion: he was not afraid of being in two or more places at once. We can be grateful that his poetry keeps a part of him here with us.

About the colorful, poignant cover: The joined hands of the "Three Great Freedom Fighters" seem to form a symbolic crossroads, a true image of the invisible. This trinity—John Brown, Harriet Tubman, and Frederick Douglass—creates a point of departure and arrival. Of course, the artist, William H. Johnson, seems to have been born at the crossroads in Florence, South Carolina. Here is a black man raised in the heart of Dixie, who ventures to New York City, to Provincetown, and then to Europe. He paints impressionistic pieces of Florence and Denmark, and then decides on portraying black Americans through a "semi-primitive" mode. The colors seem to convey a visual jazz that springs out of the 1920's into our lives today.

from In the Garden of Papa Santuzzu

The Fisherman's Son:
Teresa Pantaluna

Once there was a poor but honest man, what we call *un'omu di pazienza*, a man of patience, who worked the whole day—day after day—in the unrelenting heat of the scorching sun, casting his nets out into the blue sea, then rowing his little boat wide and far so as to make the nets stretch, then pulling them back, hand over hand, up through the dazzling water, each drop a blinding turquoise jewel, snagging barely enough fish to feed a kitten, let alone a wife and a house overflowing with daughters. The man's name was Placidu. As the father of a hundred daughters, he was most ironically named.

Did I say a hundred daughters? I meant a thousand. Hey, twenty thousand is more like it. There were so many of them it was impossible for me to keep count! I have only so many fingers and toes!

As a young man Placidu was exactly as his name suggests, as calm and unfettered as water in a stream. If there was a rock in his path, he flowed around it. When he had to row his boat against a strong tide, he apologized to each wave for upsetting its wake. He smiled at nearly everything, especially the fruit of the sea that he lifted up into his boat, until both his cheeks became creased with the dimples that all of his grandchildren inherited.

One day Placidu fell beneath a spell that couldn't be broken by prayer or potion. He discovered a secret island. On this island was a pathway twisting darkly through a thicket. The path led him through nettle and bramble, down valley and up hill, to a secret nook hidden away deep in the forest, where in the center there was a small pond that each evening at twilight filled with the glimmering figures of scores of girls bathing.

The girls frolicked in the water, shoulders glistening, long legs fluttering just below the water's surface, bottoms bobbing delightfully in the gently lapping waves. At the pond's far end, several girls washed their long dark hair beneath a cascading curtain of water. Then they dove into the pond, knifing the surface with their hands.

Each evening Placidu spied on them, squatting beside a fig tree. After a while his appetites grew so inflamed that he grabbed one of the nearby figs and squeezed it until all of its seeds spurted out onto the ground. He did this night after night, again and again and again, until the tree was nearly bare of fruit.

One evening as Placidu watched the swimmers, he grabbed the tree's last fig. As usual, in his excitement he squeezed it until it burst, but now instead of seeds the spirit of the pond leapt from his clenched hand. Placidu fell back, amazed and frightened.

The spirit was about as high as a woman's thumb. Hey, it only makes sense that you can't be too tall if you live inside a fig! But even if you're small you can still be powerful! Young Placidu had the wits to grab the spirit and command three wishes, but the clever thing twirled like a *trich-trach* until Placidu's palm throbbed with pain. This female spirit accepted no rough treatment or disrespect.

She stood on Placidu's burning palm, one hand on her hip, the other raised, like a sensible mother correcting an errant child. "You say you demand three wishes? Well, first I'll ask three questions! Where do you come from? Where are you going? What do you want?"

Placidu's head spun. He wanted only to tumble in the water with the girls, but his tongue couldn't catch the words to express his desire. As to where he was from and where he was going, he'd never given either concern much thought. So he just pointed to the pool and grinned.

Now, spirits generally aren't known for their good tempers. This spirit was particularly testy. "Silly boy," she proclaimed, "you want to frolic with these girls, and yet each night you come here and steal my fruit. Instead of splashing in the water with them, you splash the ground with my seed. All right, I'll give you something to remember me by! From this day on, from now until the day you die, I deem that each seed you spill becomes a girl just like one of these girls, and I command that you feed and clothe them and give them a place to live, a house with a tight roof and strong, thick walls and narrow windows covered with jalousies so that sneaky, empty-headed boys like you can't spy on them each evening when they're naked and at play."

Then the spirit and the girls in the pond disappeared. Placidu made his way back to his rowboat, thinking the spirit had been only one of the sea's occasional hallucinations. But the next day when he walked the twisting trail and returned to the pond he found no one there, and the day after that he saw that the pool of water had nearly dried up, and within a week there was only mud and some tender *basilicu*, which Placidu picked and chewed sadly.

The poor fisherman sorely missed his twilight adventures. One evening as he ambled back to his rowboat he saw standing in a nearby field a ewe with the eyes of a woman. Since no one else was about he coaxed the animal toward him, offering her some of the fresh *basilicu*, and then he grabbed her and rode her back. Within minutes her sides puffed up as if she were about to explode. Then the field filled with a hundred and one baby girls, each mewing hungrily for milk.

It took him all night to get them into his boat, all the next day to take them home and feed them, all night to clean them and put them to sleep, and all the next day to feed them again. The cycle spun like a whirlpool that knows no end. Soon Placidu had no time for anything else. There was always some task to do: some crying mouth to feed, some soiled face to wash, the next meal to cook, a stack of bowls to clean, some child's stinking bottom that needed wiping.

"*Semu tutti matti!*" Placidu roared, then gnashed his teeth and foamed profusely at the mouth, all the while rolling about on the floor. It was all he could say. We're all crazy. All crazy. "*Tutti matti!*" All crazy.

In short, the clever pond spirit had cursed him with a woman's outlook and life.

The girls grew, as all living things do, and Placidu's appetites swelled, as all appetites will over time, and soon the house was bursting with daughters.

"This can't go on. This has to stop," said the ewe with the eyes of a woman. "Do something, now, before I go mad." She handed Placidu a cleaver. "Here, cut it off."

Placidu took his *cosa* in his hand and stretched it on the wooden table, then raised the cleaver high over his head. Three times his arm started down, each instance halting the blade just before it could strike flesh or wood. Finally he dropped the knife on the table and went out to visit the village priest to inquire how in the world one can both be a man and at the same time remain pure.

"Why, whenever it begins to expand," the priest said, "sprinkle it with some holy water."

"Holy water?" Placidu said.

The priest nodded. "The coldest you can find."

That night Placidu carried home a jug of holy water. With each twinge of desire he sprinkled and doused himself, and though his *cosa* became as clean as Saint Joseph's lily, it still raised its head and expanded. So Placidu went back to the priest. "I did just as you said," Placidu told him.

"Just as I said?" asked the priest. "Did you kneel on a pile of acorns and beans?"

"No," Placidu said, "you said nothing about acorns and beans."

"You didn't listen," said the priest. "Before sprinkling it with holy water, you have to kneel on a pile of hard, uncooked beans and acorns."

So Placidu tried kneeling on a mound of uncooked nuts and beans, going so far as to try baskets of broken almond shells and cups of dried peas, but his efforts met with little success. Again he went back to the priest. "I did just as you said," Placidu told him.

"Did you hold out your arms as if you were being crucified?"

"No," Placidu said.

"Well," the priest said, "you have to hold out your arms for at least three hours, until they become as heavy as lead, so heavy you can hardly hold them up any longer."

"But how can I possibly splash on the holy water if I hold my arms out?" Placidu asked.

"Trust in God," said the priest. He pointed to the straw roof of his hut. "Put your faith in God, and he'll help you find a way."

Placidu obeyed for several weeks until he finally understood that there was no way to do what the priest proposed. The sheer impossibility of purity was supposed to curb his desires. So Placidu dropped his head and slipped it back into its halter. He resigned himself to his expanding household. *"Tutti matti!"* again was all he could say.

* * *

I was one of Placidu's many daughters, number eighty-nine thousand seven hundred and twenty-six. I was the stick in the bundle that snapped my papa's back. Just before the ewe with the eyes of a woman gave birth to me, Placidu proclaimed to the sun and sky and sea and earth that the very next baby to pop out from between my mamma's legs would be a boy no matter what.

The ewe dressed me in man's clothing. Everyone from leagues around came to see me, the firstborn boy of eighty-nine thousand seven hundred and twenty-six.

"He's a beautiful baby, God bless him," they all said. To ward off the evil their compliments invited, Placidu put around my neck a coral horn.

Even though the ewe bathed me herself, she noticed only what her big sad eyes had been told by her husband to see. Placidu wanted a son, so she saw me as her son. Soon I worked beside him on the sea, even though I had a pair of rosebuds on my chest and I squatted over the baron jar whenever I peed.

"Papa," I said to him one day as we let out the nets, "would your life have been any easier if you and Mamma had sons instead of daughters?"

"Tutti matti!" he answered, and by this he meant yes, what did I think, with so many extra hands to help him, he would have been extraordinarily wealthy.

"Papa," I said, "do you admit that my work is satisfying and good?"

"Tutti matti!" And by this he meant that only an idle boat blows wind into its own sails.

"Papa," I said, "then why don't we have a few thousand of my sisters out here helping, too?"

"Tutti matti! Tutti matti!" Meaning that a girl's place is inside the house beneath her mother's gaze.

"And why is that?" I asked. "Does a daughter not have two hands, just like a son? Two arms? Two legs? Two eyes, just like you and me?"

"Tutti matti!"

"What makes me a boy?" I asked. "Is it that Mamma cuts my hair? That I wear these pantaloons? That I work in the boat beside you?"

"Tutti matti!"

"Look at my hairless chin. My round hips. These apples bursting forth on my chest. Papa, am I defined by my essence or my function?"

"*Tutti matti!*"

"And if you're concerned that a girl allowed outside the house cannot be adequately protected," I asked, "what possible harm might befall her out here with you in the middle of the vast and lonely sea?"

"*Tutti matti! Tutti matti!*" he replied, looking frantically about, and by this he meant that danger lurked everywhere, and my naïve and rash words risked inviting it.

"Do you mean that some octopus or eel or stingray might swim by and spy on her?" I asked.

"*Tutti matti!*" Meaning that any man's sight might fall on her and by seeing her the man might come to crave her, and his desires might do her irreparable harm and evil, that a daughter's place was to be hidden away, to be kept inside and out of sight, locked up and away, screened, cloaked, veiled, shrouded, made secret, invisible, unseen.

"It sounds to me as if the boys rather than girls are the trouble," I said.

"*Tutti matti!*" The thickest vein on his neck throbbed wildly and appeared ready to pop.

"And yet the girls are punished and made to stay inside."

"*Tutti matti!*" Meaning that we would be wise to remember that he didn't create the world.

"So all of this is God's fault," I said, pointing up to the sky.

"*Tutti matti!*" Meaning that the gnat struggling in the web is in no place to criticize the spider.

"Particularly when the spider's a man," I declared.

"*Tutti matti! Tutti matti!*" he exclaimed, falling to his knees and beating his chest and repeatedly making the sign of the cross.

Of course we'd gone around in too narrow a circle that day to catch much more than seaweed in our nets, but I saw then how the whole system worked and how truly bad it stunk. God's will or not, this boy-girl business simply wasn't a productive or intelligent plan. I understood that rules come from community and serve the community's overall needs. To make good soup, you can't have everybody drawing water from the well. Someone's needed to chop the zucchini. But this idea of keeping my eighty-nine thousand seven hundred and twenty-five sisters locked inside the house every day seemed to me utter folly and waste.

I reminded Papa that God had originally wanted the Virgin Mary to be a *Siciliana*. God had little trouble finding an appropriate candidate—there were virgins in Sicily of every size and age—but the Almighty was unable to find a single Sicilian household where he could send in his pigeon without the bird being attacked by the girl's mother and a gang of her aunts.

"Who gave you permission to sneak in here and talk to her?" the women would shout at the bird, whacking the terrified thing to death with their brooms.

So God searched for a land with looser morals, where his feathered messenger wouldn't end up in the stew pot.

Cu nesci arrinesci.
They who leave, succeed.

Departure was my only option, disguise my only way out. A girl traveling alone was viewed as damaged goods, a cracked or broken vessel, abandoned and deserving of shame. She was prey to every vulture gliding the air above her. It was unthinkable for an unmarried girl to live apart from her family. A girl without family was considered as having no value or worth. Where was her father, her brothers, her uncles? Without men to safeguard her, the vultures would conclude that she'd done something horrible to cast dishonor on her family. Put crudely, she was a *buttana*, little more than the devil's own dirty slut.

I was the eighty-nine-thousandth seven-hundred-and-twenty-sixth daughter of a sheep whose wretched existence centered around nurturing the endless procession of bawling lambs that slid from her womb. My mother lacked the time even to wipe her own pee. There were always three or four dozen infants suckling her teats, always a few hundred more baaing something in her ear, another thousand crying for water, more thousands squalling for something to eat, still more thousands arguing over a piece of lint or the hint of shadow flitting suddenly across a wall, something so insignificant as to hardly deserve notice but that they felt required her immediate and undivided attention, so that all you could hear inside our house was the calling of "Ma! Maa! Maa!

Baa! Baa! Baa-aa!" rising to such deafening crescendos that only a saint or someone truly insane could be unaffected by the din.

Sometimes, very late at night, I'd crawl to her over the straw across all the other bodies. I'd pick fattened ticks from behind her ears and with my curled fingers comb out her matted hair. There were three or four seconds every night when everyone was silent and she could sleep. I'd pretend she was my lamb and that I was the ewe.

One night in her sleep she whispered, "I'm drowning in a sea of children," so low that I nearly thought the sound was only her breath.

"Mamma," I said, "please forgive me when I run away."

Then a few thousand of the newborns awoke and whimpered and began sucking her raw and dry, and another couple thousand had nightmares and called for her soothing touch, and over here a flock started scratching its fleas, and within a few moments it was a madhouse all over again.

No wonder Papa worked the sea! To be by one's self, in a boat out on the gray water, seemed beyond Heaven! The very thought of being alone somewhere was thrilling beyond name.

The first time that my father took me out to the sea, the silence was so loud I had to cover my ears. I put a metal pail over my head and beat it with two sticks to match the song in the house I had grown used to hearing! After a while Papa lifted the bucket from my face. We were alone in his little boat, way out on a rolling sheet of slate-gray water. Papa was explaining that this part of the Mediterranean between Sicilia and Africa was known as the African Sea. I pulled my first breath of truly fresh air into my lungs.

"*Lu Mari Africanu,*" Papa repeated, gesturing widely with his arms. He cast out the nets and began to row.

Then all at once I heard the most terrifying pounding. I clutched my ears and then my chest. My mind raced. The pounding was horrifying. I was certain I'd die.

Papa held me until I calmed down. He explained that the sound was merely the beating of my own heart.

"My own heart?" I said. I'd never heard it before. I thought he must be joking. "Papa, are you saying that I have my own heart?"

"Yes, my son," he said.

"Not my sisters' or Mamma's?"

He shook his head no.

"All my own? No one else's?"

"Entirely yours, *figghiu miu*."

I couldn't get over it. "My own heart!" I cried.

So in my jacket, pantaloons, and boots I set off for the Golden Land, where it was rumored that families didn't have eighty-nine thousand seven hundred and twenty-six daughters. As I began to hike the rocky road through the mountains to Palermu, I listened to my heart. Its steady thumping told me there was nothing I would be unable to do. I had the best of both sexes: the guile and wit of a woman, and the appearance and freedom of a man.

Understand that people see less with their eyes than with their minds. If they are told that a thing is true, they tend to adapt their vision so as to see it as such. I didn't so much pretend to be a man as forget that I was a woman. On my back were a poor villager's rough clothes. That's mainly all that people saw. I stuffed a folded handkerchief into my pantaloons to give them a better fit, but that was it for costume. My hair was short, my face tanned dark from the sea. If I pretended anything, it was that I was rich.

I realized that becoming a man isn't so much a shift in gender as it is a change in social standing or class. So I pretended to be the son of a wealthy baron, attacked by thieves and stripped of every valuable thing I owned. I lay flat on my back in a ditch beside the roadway waiting for some peasants to come along and give me aid. I filled the air with loud curses for my miserable robbers, who were so greedy they'd plucked me bare and left me only their insulting rags. I gave my jacket an extra tear or two for show. I smeared a stripe of mud on my face. Finally I heard a gang of peasants tromping up the road. I let loose a low moan and shouted loud my sad story.

As the *genti di campagna* rushed to my aid, I did as the son of a wealthy baron would and chastised them for not arriving more quickly. I called them lazy and useless and unworthy of even the air their filthy snouts breathed. Immediately I ordered them to give me water and food.

They stood about apologizing, their eyes downcast, while I ate. I made a show of tossing the crusts of their crude bread into the weeds and then had the peasants line up in a row and recite their names, villages, and occupations. Then I told them that I wished to be entertained. By now they were asking if they might carry me along the road on their broad shoulders. It's still amazing to me how easily they allowed their necks to slip into the yoke my act provided.

One man pulled a concertina from beneath his cloak. A second beat time on a tambourine. The sun shone with happy fierceness as the peasants sang.

> *The weather this day is so sharp and alive!*
> *Lord, lead me the way back to the bed of my wife,*
> *Whose fat arms and thighs give me such sweet tumbles*
> *As I shut my eyes on my life's trials and stumbles.*
> *Lord, before I'm old, return me to my family!*
> *Pockets bulging with gold after I've crossed the sea!*
> *While I still have hair and teeth!*
> *May her legs wrap me in their wreath!*
> *May her arms hold me tight!*
> *Now and through the long night!*

In Palermu I allowed the singing peasants to tell my tale to the wealthy *baruni* who crowded around us. They knew that *banditi* ruled the hills, particularly in the south. Girgenti was a place where a man didn't allow even a fly to land on his nose!

How fortunate I was to have lived, the barons' sons exclaimed, attributing my luck to my slight build, which they surmised must have posed a minimum of threat to my robbers.

I remembered to act unimpressed, pretending I was as rich as any one of these unbelievably wealthy young men. I requested nothing of them, not even a sip of cool water. I merely answered questions put to me and expressed my situation. When asked if I was tired from my journey, I sighed and said, "A bit." They then implored me to rest in someone's spacious room, where a servant brought me bread, *minestra*, meat, cheese, and wine.

I picked at the food as if its opulence didn't faze me. I sipped some soup and nibbled a piece of the cheese. Afterwards, over cigars, I told the rich sons the story of Placidu's secret island and pool and the ewe with the eyes of a woman, attributing the tale to my peasant companions. The *baruni* met my wit with laughter and applause.

They insisted that while I was in Palermu I make use of their carriages and drivers. They argued over which tailor's stitches were fine enough to fashion for me a new and proper suit of clothes. They gave me boxes of cigars and *frutta candita*. Several of the young men suggested I contact their bankers, who were instructed to advance me any sum I required. When I just so happened to mention that I'd intended to visit America, the son of an owner of one of the steamship companies gave me the name of his first captain, whom I called on the following day and who politely shook my hand and bowed before placing me *gratis* in a cabin of the finest class.

In my new clothes, in my shiny cabin, I made my way across the wide, seemingly endless sea. One morning as I strolled the rolling deck, rocked forth and back by the powerfully swelling ocean, my eyes fell on a lonely peasant, skin as dark as an olive soaked in brine, nose like the beak of a hawk, and beneath it a drooping mustache, my husband-to-be, the firstborn son Gaetanu from the province of Girgenti.

He was over in steerage walking dizzily among the cattle, clearly every bit as sick as a poisoned dog. I stared at him until his eyes caught mine. He nodded absently and out of habit, like a peasant to any *baruni*, with a sorry look on his mouth as if he were about to spit.

Perhaps it was the soot that blew in his face from the filthy smokestacks or the stench of the animals around him or his nausea from the sea. But there was something about him that gave me pause. Something about him arrested me. I felt somehow as if I were looking at another version of myself. If I'd been born a boy, I thought, I would be exactly him, not so much in appearance but in attitude. He was like my own brother, I thought, the mirror image of my soul. He was everything that I was, only undisguised and in reverse.

He wore his cap low, nearly concealing his eyes, like I'd worn mine when I fished the sea with my father. He slouched his shoulders, kept his hands in his pockets, and kicked whatever lay on the ground ahead of him, exactly in the way that I'd walked when I was waiting for something in life to happen, when I felt that nothing but more of the same lay in wait for me, when I desired sluggish fate to advance and ride on the crest of some wind of change.

Then the smoke cleared and he looked up at me, his solitary stare piercing the linen of my suit. His eyes were bright and clear. For a full moment I felt that he could see me exactly as I was: the disguised, desperate daughter of a cursed yet stubborn *piscaturi* and a wide-eyed, flea-infested, absurdly fertile ewe.

Every morning the peasant and I walked the deck trading glances until one day he paused within shouting distance and asked what village was I from. The sea raged wildly beneath us. The remaining cattle lowed continually in complaint.

My heart beat so rapidly that I could barely yell my village's name. He said he could tell I was from the southern coast by the sure-footed way that I paced the deck. I told him that my father and I had fished the African Sea for tuna and sardines.

Ahh, he said with a wistful smile. He'd never eaten sardines but he'd heard from those who had that they were delicious.

I told him the flavor of sardines held no romance, that after a few months sardines came to taste like paste. He laughed and recited the proverb, *"Lu pani di la casa stuffa."* Homemade bread grows tiresome. Then he added, "But to a mouth used to eating slugs and straw, even unromantic paste would be a feast." He tipped his cap and disappeared among the livestock.

We had a few other conversations, none long, all of them across the distance separating the ship's classes. Soon I was able to convince him to accept some of the food brought each day to my cabin. I told him that on my side of the ship, food was going to waste, and perhaps he could help me distribute it. I don't know if he ate what I gave him or if in turn he offered it to those more needy. Talking to him during the stormy passage tempted me to forget my pretense. My insides softened and grew mutable as wax.

People think the immigrant ships went directly to Ellis Island but in fact they stopped first at New York's Hudson River Pier, where the American citizens and first-class passengers departed. The immigration officials inspected me onboard ship the afternoon the ship docked.

Remember I told you that people see what their mind tells them to expect. The doctor expected to see a young Sicilian nobleman, so when he entered my cabin that's precisely what he found. For the occasion I wore a silk scarf over my vest, and I puffed a thick cigar.

The doctor apologized for the interruption and inspected my eyes and ears and felt and measured the strength of my pulse. I offered him my box of *frutta candita*. With a nod he gobbled several of the sugared fruits, then looked into my mouth and felt my neck and throat.

I asked him where in the harbor I might find a good bootblack. When we realized we didn't speak the same dialect, I mimed my question until he laughed and understood. I laughed, too, then offered him my cigars. He happily stuffed his pockets until I insisted that he keep the whole box.

I had only to unbutton my vest and pull up the back of my shirt so that he could listen to my lungs as I breathed and I was through.

"Okay," he said.

It was my first real American word. I liked the sound of it. "Okay," I replied. "*Grazie.*"

Later I took the barge to Ellis Island, where I waited for the mirror of my soul. As Gaetanu stepped from the tempestuous Great Hall, gazing about at every new thing with obvious fear and wonder, I hailed him and inquired where he was headed.

"Albany!" he replied, smiling so immensely you'd think Saint Peter had just allowed him inside the gates.

"What a coincidence!" I exclaimed. "I, too, am journeying to this Albany! Let's travel there together, okay?"

He and a dozen other unfortunates were accompanied by a pair of the *patruni*'s agents, well-fed men in American clothes. "I go with my friend, okay?" I told them. "Sure," they said, smiling at each other with their shiny gold teeth. "There's always a place for one more." They led us through a dark passageway that opened into a high-ceilinged room, inside of which stood some sort of narrow house cluttered with wide chairs and walls lined with glass windows. Gaetanu and I sat cautiously on a chair inside the house until the floor jerked forward beneath our feet. Suddenly the entire house began to move!

"May God have mercy on our souls!" Gaetanu shouted. "It's the end of the world!"

Beneath us I felt a great series of rumbling explosions, then a pair of screams or high whistles from above. Outside the glass windows, the air grew thick with smoke. I feared that a volcano had erupted. The screams must be from those trapped in its burning lava. "We'd better prepare our souls to die!" I shouted to my new friend.

We'd both fallen forward onto the back of the wide chair in front of us. I sat up and quickly raised my feet from the floor, fearing the lava that would soon pour through the moving house. Then the room filled suddenly with light and a rocky field flew past the windows, and then the field turned green with splendid grasses, and the rumbling floor beneath us clattered more evenly and quietly, rocking us now from side to side. Another pair of whistles pierced the air.

"We're in a flying house!" Gaetanu shouted.

"Perhaps," I declared, "though it may be more a roofed wagon." I decided I had to again act like a baron. "Be calm," I said in a reassuring tone. "I'm quite sure we're safe just as long as the stupid driver doesn't hit a tree."

For several minutes then we gazed out the windows, furiously watching out for oncoming trees.

The others in the wagon with us seemed unconcerned with the danger. Gaetanu imitated them and then sat back, relaxed.

He stared out the windows at the houses and fields. After a while he said, "Look how the flowers grow gracefully beside the other flowers, the thorns and weeds in the ditch beside the other thorns and weeds."

"Yes," I said. "I see."

"Likes with likes. The same with the same." He knocked the first fingers of his hands together. "See, they don't mix like you and me."

"A *piscaturi* such as me knows nothing of flowers," I replied.

"Yet the fisherman's son travels across the sea in a cabin of the highest class."

"Only a fool judges wine by its bottle," I said. I showed him the callouses on my hands. "Feel," I said. "My hands are every bit as hard as yours. Would a stranger to labor have hands like these?"

As he traced his fingertips across my palms I grunted and pulled my hands away, as one man would with another, yet inside

I felt a hot blush rise in my throat and cheeks. I slapped his shoulder and laughed. "Trust me, my friend," I said heartily.

"My friend," he said, eyes twinkling, nodding and slapping my shoulder hard in return.

Still he continued to test me, asking me if I rode and, if so, how I sat on the horse's back, whether I held the reins with one or both hands, and with which hand I used the whip. I straddled the seat, knees apart, my right hand holding imaginary reins, my left threatening with the whip. He asked me the proper direction to pull a razor over one's whiskers, whether it's preferable to go with the grain of the beard or against it. I said that for the best shave one draws the razor against the beard's grain after first wetting the hairs with scented water. Then he asked me why, if in truth I were as rich as my clothes, its pockets were even more empty than his.

I squeezed the cloth that I'd stuffed in my pantaloons and laughed and said, "A dozen maidens between the coast and Palermu would swear that my pockets weren't empty."

"Only a dozen?" he said with a laugh. "On my walk to Palermu I'm sure I had three times more." He gave the prominent thickness in his pants a slight squeeze, then elbowed me sharply in the ribs. "Tell me, my friend, what does a man of your class whisper to the girls before you lay with them?"

"Of course I tell them that I love them, the same as you say to the girls whom you meet, only three times less often," I replied.

He nodded. "And what do they say to you in return?"

"Why, of course they echo the same words as had been mine, only three times less loud."

He nodded a second time. "And afterwards, what words do you utter as you depart?"

"Of course I say that someday I'll return, just as you tell all those whom you meet and who love you, only three times less sadly."

His mood grew serious then. "In truth," he said, "on the road to Palermu I lay with nothing more gentle than the jagged tips of rocks, nothing more generous than hardship."

"May both mistresses be stingy to us," I said, "now and forever."

"So be it." He nodded a third time. "After all, we're on our way to Albany!"

"Paradise," I said. "The New Eden. The Golden Land."
"*La Merica!*" Gaetanu exclaimed to all seated on the train.

God's blood, the factory in Albany where my Tannu was to work off his debt to the *patruni* was more like Hell.

Blinding fires taller than a house crackled and blazed within end-less rows of yawning ovens. The golden flames twisted and writhed in insatiable hunger as the workers scrambled in subservience like ants on a log. Everywhere huge machines roared in an eternally thumping, pounding, ear-splitting din that knew no end. All of this chaos was contained by the factory's dark, unbroken walls, held down by the ceiling that blocked any breeze or sunlight, so that all the air we pulled into our lungs was stifled and suffocating, wrung dry of any goodness or freshness, tainted by smoke and soot and the fetid smell of grease and metal mixed with oil.

How can people go from working their entire lives out in God's air and sunlight, in his heat and cold, his clear and rain, his bright and cloudy, his calm and windy, to being cut off from all sense of the day's nature? Oh, how I missed the forgiving openness of the African Sea! To be laboring alongside my father, letting out the day's nets while reciting our prayers for the Lord's bounty, now seemed a faint dream to me. What mistake had I made coming to this tortured land?

For the first months Gaetanu and I shared a tiny room, living as two men. We slept on the same bed, like monks, feet to head, collapsing on the narrow cot nearly the moment we came in from our day's labors. Then after an hour or so we'd rise and eat, main-ly *pani e favi*, a piece of bread big as my fist and a small bowl of beans, along with whatever greens we could find and afford. I washed on the sly after he was asleep, in the women's bathhouse, avoiding all the various traps that might reveal me. Each month I was careful to hide the bright evidence that I was daughter num-ber eighty-nine thousand seven hundred and twenty-six.

Gaetanu worried constantly about his debt. He was smart in the way of all *campagnoli* but was absolutely witless and thick when it came to numbers. Pencils and tablets of paper terrified him. I tried teaching him how to count on his fingers, but he fre-quently confused directions and in the midst of calculation would end up taking away part of what he'd intended to add, or adding half of what he was supposed to take away, so that by the time his reckonings were finished he was usually exactly where he had started. Then he would argue with me that his wrong answer was correct and that all calculation and mathematical process were absurd and meaningless.

He'd spend endless hours trying to convince me that one plus zero equaled zero. He would start with one finger raised on his hand, then transfer it to the other, making his first hand into a fist, juggling the one raised finger back and forth, all the while asking me if his addition was correct, until he'd use the one raised finger to count the number remaining on his other hand, which of course always was zero.

Gaetanu was extraordinarily fond of zero. He said it was the most fascinating number because it was so unlike the others, something and yet not something all at the same time. He said that here in the New Land very often he felt the same way.

"In Sicilia I used to be something," he'd say, raising a finger, "but here I feel just like this," pointing the finger at his other, empty fist.

He liked to hold up one fist and ask me how much.

"Zero," I'd answer.

"No," he'd say, "one," and shake his head and point to his fist.

And if I answered one, he'd point to his absence of raised fingers and say zero. Then we'd argue.

To silence his senselessness I'd start counting. Daughter of a most prolific mother, I was born with an appreciation for numbers! I'd grown up literally counting sheep! I knew just how high numbers were able to climb!

But Gaetanu would refuse to listen to me. He'd repeat the contradiction of his raised fist and his justification that one plus zero equaled zero, claiming that these additions explained how he had journeyed all this way and had still gotten nowhere and was in fact even more poor now than he'd been before.

No one could argue against that conclusion. In truth, after the first year he was in an even deeper hole of debt to the *patruni*.

One hot summer night as we lay in bed discussing these arithmetics, the air grew so thick and heavy it was a great labor just to take the next breath. Neither of us could sleep. The humid night stretched itself endlessly before us. We tossed on the mattress until his hands happened to brush against my hips. He was arguing with me about the number ten, claiming that all sensible arithmetic must stop there, that no number could ascend higher than ten because ten tumbled back to zero before it could possibly reach the height of elevenness and as a result might as well be merely one, so that at the second he touched my hips, the fingers of both his hands were stretched forward.

Then a bolt of lightning shot through the sky, transforming the inky darkness into a clear moment of day. A cool wind surged through the room. A curtain of rain smacked the street below our window with a steady *shhhhhhh,* and darkness mercifully fell again over us as his ten fingers drifted from my hips toward the front of my pantaloons.

"Tell me your name," he whispered in the darkness. I could barely hear him, the rain was pounding the roof with such force. "Your name," he said in a deeper voice. "Tell me your true and real woman's name."

The lightning bolt had transformed him into a bull. I stroked his thick shoulders and then his forehead, careful not to hurt my hands against his sharp, upturned horns.

He scrambled from the bed and stood, pawing the floor with his front hoof, then stretched back the bulk of his powerful neck and bellowed loudly in the night.

As I changed myself back into a woman, I told him all he needed to know.

Adriatic

She wakes, alone, on the cruise ship's highest deck,
lying in a chair, beneath the night.
Despite his promises, he isn't there.
The night is cool with patchy, floating fog;
the ship, deserted, seems to drift without
direction. Tonight, she'd rushed into Brindisi,
the harbor city of pestilence and quakes,
and bought her ticket and rushed onboard.

Now drifting on the silent seas alone,
she wonders if she bought the proper passage.
Drifting south and east, she doesn't really care.
She might arrive in Corinth, maybe not.
She dreams of Crete and Rhodes, Izmir,
and Haifa...even Alexandria.
It doesn't really matter; she feels content—
as if she's slowly drifting in the right direction.

Touch the Blues

Say I'm a man of fifty-three years,
flexible in my thinking, yet shaped
by certain heavily reinforced concepts
about my relationship with the world.

Say I'm someone who cannot speak seriously
for long without blurting a phrase,
some winking word curve that proclaims
I'm ready to ride pleasure
all the way to reverence.

Okay, I'm alone, stepping carefully down
metal stairs to a blues
club above a river in England. It's smoky,
and dark.
            Keeping my eye on the piano player, because
he's playing brilliantly, and because the small stage
is a source
of light, I fumble blindly
for a table.
            I'm convinced if I look toward the music
I will find my way.
            Settled then into a chair, I discover
with pleasure I'm not alone here. Her face glows
with the blues.
            A shiver
of recognition ripples through
my chest. Despite
a growing intimacy, I begin the usual
mental listing of setbacks
                        until the sax lays down a moan.
Shaking her head, my stranger
says, "It's okay.

Don't." She moves
her hand,
      her naked skin
toward mine,
         and her voice gives birth
to the kind of phrase
that changes you:
         "Choose this chance
to touch me."

Art Pepper

I keep seeing him as the tiny chill
of sound rising out of a black groove,
this record and its mist of scratches,

and imagine it would have pleased him,
to think he could escape this planet alive.
Or the other notion, how he is more

needle than sound, that a piece of him
lies down still: you can feel it sinking,
tapering into the music he's in.

Each phrase is a kind of vein that way,
a small bruise swelling on its vine.
Music, he said, would keep him young.

And it did. With every song a pilot
sleeping at the speed of light. True,
there were nights to survive, so many

rituals that fixed him to his body
they seemed like another man's life to him:
a thin face floating in a hot spoon.

It became his memento mori, this face,
slipping in and out of its locket,
growing thinner by the year. And always

his return to the same still pool,
the white translucent throats of syringes
blushing briefly in the aftermath.

In the end it was his own blood
he shot, however foreign, newly tainted.
It became his second wind, a chaser.

See, you can cheat death, he said leaning
into the mike (they could have been anyone
in the dark, listening) then he blew

a pip of air into his sax to clear it.
It must have sent a shiver through the crowd,
as if to play this freely took a streak

of thievery or spite—he split his lip
to prove it—or that music were a black market,
a sting, the way he winged it over changes,

taking apart the heads of tunes in fakebooks.
What he played best and longest he closed
his eyes to hear, as if darkness made him

more permeable to sound, more absorbent
like a black plate standing in the sun.
Death deserved him after all, having come

so near...at least he thrived to think so,
amazed to live so deep into the red,
to pass the loan shark of his last day,

though the future kills no one and is
nowhere and knows nothing of the moment
in the back of a cab when a startled vein

broke in his cortex and he looked up
at his wife's face, struck by her panic,
slowly lapsing into the numbness of her arms.

Who alive can resist the next thing,
what it was to drown in himself, rushed
from a world of strange affections, all

those heads with his saxophone in them,
at the record store, say, where a man might
flip through a bin of releases and pause

to listen, half-blinded by the sheer speed
of joy, the stillness at the heart of it,
the music welling up like blood in his brain.

The Feather at Breendonck

I am praying again, God—pale God—
   here, between white sky and snow,
by the larch I planted last spring, with one branch
   broken at the elbow. I pick it up,

wave winter away: I do things like that,
   call the bluebirds back, throwing yarn
and straw in the meadow, and they do come,
   so terribly blue, their strangled *teoo-teoo*

echoing my prayer: *Dieu, Dieu*—
   the same *Dieu* who stained the feather
I found in the barbed fields of the Breendonck
   Concentration Camp, near Antwerp, in 1952.

My father tried to slap it out of my hand: "It's filthy,"
   but I held on to it—I knew it was an angel's.
"They only killed a few Jews here," he said,
   "eight, nine hundred, maybe."

So I wave their angels away with my feather,
   away from my father, away from the terribly
blue skies over the Breendonck Canal, where barges loaded
   bricks for Antwerp, where my father loaded ships

for Rotterdam, Bremerhaven, and Hamburg—
   and the port expanded, and Antwerp grew,
and his business flourished, and he kept on repeating:
   "That's all we needed: a good war."

         for Eleanor Wilner

Letter from the North

for B.W. and P.T.D.

In wet fields the farmers' cramped
hands clutch fast to their hoes.
We tumble through stone-colored flesh.
All night the plane floating up over the oceans,
unknown lives passing through us.
So many. Barely enough time to say the names.
Gone, as if taken by a huge gray
hand entering a station, or those boats
with makeshift heads
nosing the stairs by the river.
This morning I turned the corner at Bui Thi Xuan
and walked into a funeral. The great black
bus without doors sailed past me,
the white banded mourners, red flags
leading drummers to the lake.
What is it we have seen
that we must travel so far to pray?

On Mai Hac De last night
I sat with the old men
in the slow dripping rain
and watched the cards fall in the dark.
Someone called my name,
I turned too late.
The gate creaked closed, a shadow
moving in the smoke of the kerosene lamp.
Outside the Apocalypse Bar, tourist buses
lined up on their way to the snake restaurant.
A young girl and her brother huddled in jackets
over a charcoal fire. They offered their warmth for sale.
A wooden bench, brandy, Laotian tobacco, strong tea.
Mutes, I sat and watched them sign in the darkness,

faces screwed up into those unsayable syllables,
bodies twisting, arms turned up, bent like ancient
wrestlers or those gods carved on old temple ceilings,
or the humpbacked man, two birds on his shoulders
by the yellow wall at Tran Quoc Pagoda.
On Hang Vai St., the wedding procession
stopped to light fireworks.
In the narrow street of restaurants, rockets
flew up in the air, drawing whole families out
to see the hissing snakes' heads of the flares,
the green and yellow sparks falling on tin rooftops.
Ba Chu Lieu, she came in a red dress first.
At her shrine I watched a soldier
burn money in a pit for his lost companions.
Time, he said. That's all.
In the story everyone already knew
the young girl was Lan Co, the old King's daughter.
The third time she came she was dressed in white at Ho Tay.
This is what my friend told me in the small boat
that took us there, boat rocking in the misty waters,
the early morning fog, the great fields of birds spread
like beggars' fingers calling from the lake.
Oh my friends, if they keep coming
I think their shadows will make a bridge
even our poor souls could cross.

The Death of Jazz

Late June, dusk in Paris,
a man found you, unaccompanied,
on a park bench. Slouched,
chin on chest, gaze fixed
at the brick fountain, its white
tumbling spires, you
were the man from the night before.
At the concert hall, you'd played
that long instrument, lean
and ebony with silver keys,
like a stretched saxophone, yet
something else. A bass clarinet,
brilliant and rich, you cried its voice
into every register, soaring and sinking
its song. The man touched your shoulder.

I must have sugar, the plea
so genuine he helped you up, into his car
and down streets scanning for a
confectionery, headlights freeing
for seconds from the falling darkness
doors, windows, awnings of this city
you'd see gray for the last time.
When the car stopped you were silent.
Melody, the beat of your own heart,
nectar of your veins turned against you
pulsed your ears. The man tapped the bar,
its gold wrapper, against the window
and you lifted your hand forgetting glass.
He drove you home with the murmur
of your address in broken French, soft
nougat at your lips, two failing sighs:
Please and *Joyce.*

Next day you felt better, though
yesterday, was it real?
You'd seen the fountain dance, water
churn into strange nudes, writhing up
and crashing down in glittering circles.
You could make Berlin.
The date was arranged, it was just a matter
of going. Sweat beaded your brow.
Didn't she see? For the first time you were
booked solid, six months, they knew you,
were awaiting you, and her eyes could only
fill with worry. You pulled at your beard,
smiled, said her name.
It would be all right.

Hard to move your arms
and legs, they got you to your room.
Black and American, a musician,
they figured heroin, and this your
private business. If they'd known you
in Los Angeles, still at home, in Roy Porter's band—
twenty-one, full of learning, cheeks a deep chestnut
vibrant as your eyes, days rooted
so firmly in the life of sound you had no
need for needles, interest in glass lips
of booze or women—they would have thought twice,
puzzled over your room service request:
six-pack of cola, half gallon of vanilla ice cream,
trays of ice. Blood gone bad, shirt
wet to your skin, you faltered to open a window.
Sleep, someone offered in English.

Your flute was lightest
and you brought it out instead of
the clarinet or saxophone.
Half-trot, you made it past the piano,
the bassist, drummer waiting—all so eager,
this their first chance to test themselves
against the vinyl they'd dulled, stylus

they'd lifted back, over and over
to the platter's edge, studying and
perplexing at your solos—now here, in person,
and you were attempting only to balance
the fumbling motion of your body.
You tried, strove to place your fingers
over the keys, and fell.

One long minute the hall
fell silent. The first whisper
made another, glance became gesture enough
to rise and, slowly, the audience
moved to leave, shoulders
bumping awkward filing toward the exit.
You were gone, your body soon meaningless
somewhere in the white halls of the public hospital,
nurses and physicians bothering over
something come too far.
Three lingered, their instruments
dumb on the stage. They talked
briefly and quietly, removed the flute
from the floor. Later, each took a long way home,
once inside, desklight on against darkness,
made some kind of prayer, spent one private moment
to know, in no small part,
this death as more.

RICHARD CECIL

In Search of the Great Dead

In Paris, Vallejo's hotel
near the Bibliothèque Nationale
charges a hundred a night,
and Ginsberg's seedy room
on the rue Git-le-coeur
sports flowered wallpaper now,
and a couple of Michelin stars.
Cabourg's Grand Hôtel
on the chilly Normandy coast,
nearly driven from business
by the sunny "costas" of Spain,
rents "Chambre Marcel Proust"
for twice the price of a suite—
a week's pay for the profs
who book it, months in advance,
to lie in Proust's bed one night
fighting sleep as they read
his description of insomnia
in his snail-paced masterpiece.
And, speaking of Spain, in Ronda
Rilke slept for a month
in Room 208
of the Reina Victoria Hotel,
which exhibits souvenirs—
some scribbles, a canceled bill—
that cold man left behind
when he resumed his search
for gorgeous emptiness
hollow as his hollow heart.
But if their names have jacked
ridiculously the rent
of the tiny, outmoded rooms
they slept in for pocket change,

like the "Taube" in Hemingway's Shruns,
now a first-class Austrian inn
with a three-color brochure
where, for $2.50 a night,
he polished *The Sun Also Rises,*
abandoned his wife for his mistress,
and blamed it all on Dos Passos—
consider visiting their tombs.

In Cimetière Père-Lachaise
in Paris you can stand
for nothing by Alice B. Toklas's
and Gertrude Stein's remains
and stare at their blank stone—
not a single word but their names
after thousands of pages of chatter!
From their excellent address
in the capital city of death,
avenues of genius
fan in all directions.
But if you prefer the lonely
and isolated dead,
Châteaubriand in St. Malo
on an island linked to the mainland
for an hour at ebb tide
rests within the sound
of the wind and the sea—and the tourists
who photograph his inscription
quick! before the causeway floods.
Then they board the ferry
to the sullen Irish coast
to add William Butler Yeats
to their album of poets' tombs.
Graves's grave's in Majorca
near the Chopin/Sand Condominiums;
Dante's is in Ravenna,
Keats's and Shelley's in Rome,
where poets and Caesars lie
whose marble cenotaphs

barbarians burned for lime.
Augustus paid Virgil and Horace
to praise his empire and Virtue,
then Nero slaughtered Lucan
for winning a poetry contest,
and Seneca for hating vice,
but all of their tombs are lost.
There is no place to stand
feeling your heart expand
at the greatness of the waste
that lies between you and them;
at the brilliance of their lines
through centuries of patronage
and hostility alike.
First the houses they lived in,
then their houses of death
disappeared, and all that's left
are their works—some of their works—
some fragment of their works.
Half of Livy's *History,*
the juiciest parts of Tacitus
were ripped out, charred, scraped off
to make paper for another bible
or wipe the ass of a monk.
All that's left of Sappho
is several hundred words
caught drifting on the wind
from the fire at Alexandria,
and *Gilgamesh,* written on stone,
is written on pebbles now—
pebbles displayed like diamonds
for crowds at the British Museum.

When the pebbles become grains of sand
and blow away in the wind
of a nuclear strike on London
or the gentler breeze of erosion
after the city's abandoned,
that epic's only remnant

will be Hatred of Death,
which is the theme of *Gilgamesh*
and also the impulse that drove
its author to hack it in granite.
"Now I'll never die,"
he said to himself as he wiped
his bleeding hands on his shirt.
And he hasn't, quite, yet,
though bombs from the War for Oil
rocked his ancient, anonymous bones
recently and will again.
The little wars and the Big One
the lovers of death are planning
will leave no monuments
but rubble and rows and columns
of identical soldiers' tombs
next to the fields and trees
or featureless, shifting dunes
that thousands of x's and y's
died for, not guessing why,
and the unmarked humps of mass graves
of civilians who got in the way.
These, too, attract their visitors,
veterans and survivors
who've vowed never to forget,
and, later, politicians
for a century or two, but at last
only the haters of death
walk these bone yard acres
shaking their heads and digging
their nails into their palms,
driving needles of pain
up their arms into their brains
to shake the drowsy numbness
of so much nameless slaughter,
exactly like the numbness
that comes, reading Livy's *History*
in bed, late at night.
Ten thousand Carthaginians

slaughtered ten thousand Romans
in 300 B.C. or vice versa—
annihilating armies
annihilated in turn
until the Empire, secured,
turned upon itself
and Romans murdered Romans—
fathers, sons, brothers—
for four more hundred years.
Their civil war graveyards,
long buried by barbarians,
must once have looked like ours
at Fredericksburg and Shiloh,
where every numbered marker
listing Company and Regiment
whispers, like Emily Dickinson,
"I'm Nobody—are you
Nobody, too?"

                   Oh, yes,
I'm Nobody, too. My plot,
reserved for a small down payment
at Valhalla Memory Gardens,
isn't a pilgrimage site;
it's not on the tour bus route,
not topped with a simple stone
carved with memorable words,
waiting, impatient, for me
to die to make them immortal.
My house, 912 East First,
lacks a bronze inscription
screwed into its plastic siding,
and will certainly be converted
to a rental, not a museum
when I leave it dead or, alive,
determined to die in Florida
or Southern France, like Yeats,
desiring a year in the sun
after a lifetime of gloom

and greenness and peasant neighbors.
That year's when I plan to write
my deathless epitaph
and enter it in the contest
glutted with Baby Boom poets
dying at the rate they were born.
But first, I'll waste my life,
like now, writing against
the grain of drowsiness—
I rose at four a.m.—
with Olive, my black and white cat,
kneading my arm with her claws—
a pleasure so much like pain,
a pain so much like pleasure,
like dying after a long illness,
then haunting the house you lived in,
brushing the fabrics you touched,
shoving ghostly feet into shoes,
marveling at their size and weight,
in which you once walked like a giant.
For even the greatest dead,
if death isn't just dirt in the mouth,
must moan with their reedy voices
for the life they lost to be famous.

BRUCE COHEN

Escaping God

When you shut your eyes to daydream, you're really
imagining the face of God, who, in the fifties, assumed
the face of Mrs. Oshkenozi, who sat in her apartment
window handing glasses of tap water to boys
in pursuit of perfect stickball. Grandpa & his
compatriots puffed unfiltered Camels & flirted

with imperfect hands of gin, downing iced vodka
& pickled herring. Out of geographical ignorance
he invented a new ocean from Minsk
to a dank tailor shop on the Lower East Side.
To this day, no male in my kin can decipher a road map.
My own father, for instance, circled the back roads

of Georgia three sweltering days past the same billboard
boasting giant alligators & the sweetest peaches,
wasting our one family vacation. Even to ask
directions violates the foundation of our religion.
Youth should bum around till their notions arrive.
The topic of my grandmother's voyage to America

was bananas, how she ate one, peel & all.
I can't erase the image, a beautiful Polish girl
in a coarse sepia dress vomiting over the rails,
praying to no God in particular.
My own sons never met this generation,
so we cart them to my cousin's kid's bar mitzvah

whose wife ditched him for another woman,
but that's a story I'll keep with the family silverware.
I believe in everything so practice nothing,
thank Mrs. Oshkenozi, who became God in the Camps

& believed in nothing so practiced kindness.
A New Age Berkeley doctor convinced us circumcision

has no medical basis, so my boys, my mother scolded,
can't be buried in a Jewish cemetery because
they have more skin on their dicks than their ancestors.
Jewish men are eternal optimists, cutting off an inch
as soon as life begins. Once as a boy I heard a glass
of water drop from a window. "Mrs. Oshkenozi, is that you?"

"For once," she said, "let's pretend it isn't to see what happens."
She read too much Malamud, which reminds me,
I'm strangely proud Grandpa was forced to read
in secret, that my father made no secret about not reading,
when he died, I was relieved I wouldn't have to be a Jew anymore.
My middle son is my father reincarnated—perpetual scam

coated in human skin, a notion no one has come up with yet.
We're the only Jews in our town. My wife, who isn't,
is obliged each winter to construct a little talk about the origins
of our faith to the elementary school. She brings the tops
& chocolate money, teaches a few songs. How everything
is based on a miracle, the comfort of not having to explain,

like a light burning longer than it should. In my house,
the unknowable generational beauty of each son
wearing his brother's hand-me-down pajamas...
Overlap becomes custom elevated to religion. Or just a mistake,
confusing one son for another, which is my concept of God.
Often, without thinking, I call him by the wrong name...

Bad Impression

Right now the men put aside
    their composing sticks
and settle by the hellbox
    chatting in groups
that never seem to vary
    from day to day.
Naturally I'm anxious to fit
    in naturally,
to be considered one amongst
    metal men and composers.
I hesitate on the edge of
    the company, not sure
which group I should join,
    not wanting to be
part wholly of any. I stroll up
    to the nearest set.
My heart pistons as fast
    as a printing machine's
and my legs are as heavy
    as a case of spacers.
It's worse than approaching some
    crush on a Saturday night
to ask her for a dance
    over the disco music
that's louder than the machine floor
    in full swing.
I blurt out about
    how Cork Celtic
will kill Hibs next Sunday
    down the Box—
In the same breath I address one comp
    as the Pele of composers.

He slowly turns and I see myself
   inverted and broken
in the mirrors of his eyes
   and in all the other eyes
turned my way, justified with his.
   He turns back and continues
what he was saying, but not
   before dumping the stick
of a wisecrack they all guffaw at.
   The other backs turn
back and I'm stranded
   like an orphan line.

But now I'm not there anymore,
   and it's years later.
I'm older than many
   of those galley slaves were then.
I walk up to the word-man
   I admire and he turns away
in such a fashion.
   His party laughs at his crack
like the typesetters,
   except, they sip from wineglasses,
instead of chipped mugs, grasp slim
   volumes and never utter a foul word.
Nevertheless they all turn
   aside or completely away
like mirrors turned to the wall
   when someone has died.

Invisible Dreams

"La poésie vit d'insomnie perpétuelle."
—Rene Char

There's a sickness in me. During
the night I wake up & it's brought

a stain into my mouth, as if
an ocean has risen & left back

a stink on the rocks of my teeth.
I stink. My mouth is ugly, human

stink. A color like rust
is in me. I can't get rid of it.

It rises after I
brush my teeth, a taste

like iron. In the
night, left like a dream,

a caustic light
washes over the insides of me.

*

What to do with my arms? They
coil out of my body

like snakes; they
branch & spit.

I want to shake myself
until they fall like withered

roots; until
they bend the right way—

until I fit in them,
or they in me.

I have to lay them down as
carefully as an old wedding dress,

I have to fold them
like the arms of someone dead.

The house is quiet; all
night I struggle. All

because of my arms,
which have no peace!

*

I'm a martyr, a girl who's been dead
two thousand years. I turn

on my left side, like one comfortable
after a long, hard death.

The angels look down
tenderly. "She's sleeping," they say

& pass me by. But
all night, I am passing

in & out of my body
on my naked feet.

*

I'm awake when I'm sleeping & I'm
sleeping when I'm awake, and no one

knows, not even me, for my eyes
are closed to myself.

I think I am thinking I see
a man beside me, & he thinks

in his sleep that I'm awake
writing. I hear a pen scratch

a paper. There is some idea
I think is clever: I want to

capture myself in a book.

*

I have to make a
place for my body in

my body. I'm like a
dog pawing a blanket

on the floor. I have to
turn & twist myself

like a rag until I
smell myself in myself.

I'm sweating; the water is
pouring out of me

like silver. I put my head
in the crook of my arm

like a brilliant moon.

*

The bones of my left foot
are too heavy on the bones

of my right. They
lie still for a little while,

sleeping, but soon they
bruise each other like

angry twins. Then
the bones of my right foot

command the bones of my left
to climb down.

MARK DOTY

Mercy on Broadway

Saturday, Eighth and Broadway,
a dozen turtles the color of crushed mint

try for the ruby rim
of a white enamel bowl

on the sidewalk, wet jade
jewel cases climbing two

or three times the length
of their bodies toward heaven

till the slick sides of the bowl
send them sliding back into

their brothers' bright heap
of grassy armament. The avenue's

a high wall of what the clubs call
deep house mix: tribal rave

from the flea market across the street,
some deejay hawking forty-five-minute sides

of pure adrenalin, snarl and sputter
and staccato bass of traffic and some idling taxi,

siren wail's high arc over it all,
blocks away, and the call and response

of kids on both sides of the avenue,
some flashing ripple of Motown sparking

the whole exhaust-shimmered tapestry
like gold thread *don't forget*

the Motor City and even some devotees'
hare rama droned in for good measure

in the sheer seamless scrim
of sound this town is, so at first

I can't make out the woman
beside me saying *You want buy turtle?*

I don't want any one of this
boiling bowl of coppery citizens

longing for release—a dozen maybe,
or nothing at all. So much to want

in this city, the world's bounty
laid out, what's the point in owning

any one piece of it? Deep house mix:
these hip-hop kids disappearing

into huge jackets and phat jeans,
these Latin girls with altarpiece earrings

gleaming like church, homo boys
eyeing each other's big visible auras

of self-consciousness all the way
across Broadway, vendors from Senegal

Hong Kong and Staten Island selling
incense sweatshirts peanuts

roasted in some burning sugar syrup.
What do you want right now?

What can't the city teach you
to want? It's body atop body here,

lovely and fragile armor dressed up
as tough, it's so many beats there's

something you can dance to, plan on it,
flash and hustle all up and down

this avenue. Don't let it fool you,
grief's going down all over

these blocks, invisible only
because indifferent and ravenous

Broadway swallows it all,
a blowsy appetite just as eager

to eat you as to let you go;
maybe you're someone in particular

but no offense pal no one's necessary
to the big sound of the avenue's

tribal, acid mix.
I'm standing here bent

over this bowl of turtles—
green as Asia, sharp-edged

as lemon grass—and ruthless
as I know this street is

nowhere, nowhere to run to,
nowhere to hide this morning there's no place

I'd rather be than smack in the thrall
of Broadway's merciless matter

and flash, pulse and trouble. *Turtle?*
You want? Their future can't be bright;

what's one live emerald clutch-purse
in the confusion and glory

Manhattan is? Listen, I've seen fever
all over this town, no mercy, I've seen

the bodies I most adored turned to flame
and powder, my shattered darlings

a clutch of white petals lifted
on the avenue's hot wind:

last night's lottery tickets,
crumpled chances blown in grates

and gutters. I'm forty-one years old
and ready to get down

on my knees to a kitchen bowl
full of live green. I'm breathing here,

a new man next to me who's beginning
to matter. *It's gonna take a miracle*

sings any one of the untraceable radios
or tape decks or personal hookups to the music

of the spheres threading this fluid
and enormous crowd *to make me love*

someone new. I don't think these turtles
are going to make it, but what

does that mean? Maybe a gleaming hour
on Broadway's jewel enough.

Unthinkably green now, they're inseparable
from the sudden constellation

of detail the avenue's become
—this boulevard continuously radiant,

if only we could see it—live integers
of this streaming town's

lush life. As you and I are, boy,
laughing and strolling and taking our parts

in its plain vulgar gorgeousness,
its cheap and shining aspirations.

I want what everybody wants,
that's how I know I'm still

breathing: deep mix, rapture
and longing. Let me take your arm,

in that shiny blue jacket I love,
clear plastic pendants hung

like bijoux from its many zippers,
let me stand close to you in the way

the avenue allows, let the sun flash
on your chrome ring, let me praise

your sideburns and your black baseball cap,
signifying gestures that prove

gonna take a miracle we're living.
I've been lucky; I've got a man

in my head who's spirit and ash
and flecks of bone now, and a live one

whose skin is inches from mine.
I've been granted this reprieve,

and I'll take whatever part
Broadway assigns me: Man on His Knees

Beside a Bowl of Turtles, Man on the Sidewalk
with His Heart in His Mouth? Let's walk,

let's drink this city street's
deep mix: ashes and altitude,

scorch and glory, its human waves
of style and talk, its hundred thousand ways to say

Hey. I looked into that shiny cup
of ambulant green and I thought

Somebody's going to live through this.
Suppose it's you? Whatever happens to me,

to us, somebody's going to ride out
these blasted years, somebody if I'm still lucky

years from now will read this poem and walk
on Broadway. Broadway's no one,

and Broadway lasts. Here's the new hat,
the silhouette of the hour. Here's the new jewelry

everybody's wearing, the right haircut,
the new dance, the new song, the next step,

the new way of walking, the world that's on
everyone's lips, the word that's on its way:

our miracle Broadway, our hour.

Night Train

I had been awake
since balmy Tokyo
on a train from lights
of pornographic neon
to places in silent mountains
I will never see again.
Across from me in the sleeper
an old man undressed
the veins in his legs
looked like green lightning
in hairless, gold skin.
He wrapped himself in a robe
moved his feet into slippers
then offered me a cigarette
and a sandwich wrapped in cellophane.
I took both, then handed him
my map, asked my slow questions.
In the end all we could do was laugh.
I lay awake in the compartment
listening to the clanging beat
of the wheels on the rails
count away time.
Asian hills peaked monstrous
and empty stations slipped
into an unthinkable distance
outside the iced windows.

Thanksgiving

This was the first Thanksgiving with my wife's family,
sitting at the stained pine table in the dining room.
The wood stove coughed during her mother's prayer:
Amen and the gravy boat bobbing over fresh linen.
Her father stared into the mashed potatoes
and saw a white battleship floating in the gravy.
Still staring at the mashed potatoes, he began a soliloquy
about the new Navy missiles fired across miles of ocean,
how they could jump into the smokestack of a battleship.
"Now in Korea," he said, "I was a gunner and the people there
ate *kimch'i,* and it really stinks." Mother complained that no one
was eating the creamed onions. *"Eat, Daddy."* The creamed onions
look like eyeballs, I thought, and then said, "I wish I had missiles
like that." Daddy laughed a 1950's horror-movie mad-scientist laugh,
and told me he didn't have a missile, but he had his own cannon.
"Daddy, eat the candied yams," Mother hissed, as if he were
a liquored CIA spy telling secrets about military hardware
to some Puerto Rican janitor he met in a bar. "I'm a toolmaker.
I made the cannon myself," he announced, and left the table.
"Daddy's family has been here in the Connecticut Valley since 1680,"
Mother said. "There were Indians here once, but they left."
When I started dating her daughter, Mother called me a half-black,
but now she spooned candied yams on my plate. I nibbled
at the candied yams. I remembered my own Thanksgivings
in the Bronx, turkey with *arroz y habichuelas* and *plátanos,*
and countless cousins swaying to *bugalú* on the record player
or roaring at my grandmother's Spanish punchlines in the kitchen,
the glowing of her cigarette like a firefly lost in the city. For years
I thought everyone ate rice and beans with turkey at Thanksgiving.
Daddy returned to the table with a cannon, steering the black
iron barrel. "Does that cannon go boom?" I asked. "I fire it
in the backyard at the tombstones," he said. "That cemetery bought
up all our farmland during the Depression. Now we only have

the house." He stared and said nothing, then glanced up suddenly,
like a ghost had tickled his ear. "Want to see me fire it?" he grinned.
"Daddy, fire the cannon after dessert," Mother said. "If I fire
the cannon, I have to take out the cannonballs first," he told me.
He tilted the cannon downward, and cannonballs dropped
from the barrel, thudding on the floor and rolling across
the brown braided rug. Grandmother praised the turkey's thighs,
said she would bring leftovers home to feed her Congo Gray parrot.
I walked with Daddy to the backyard, past the bullet holes
in the door and his pickup truck with the Confederate license plate.
He swiveled the cannon around to face the tombstones
on the other side of the backyard fence. "This way, if I hit anybody,
they're already dead," he declared. He stuffed half a charge
of gunpowder into the cannon, and lit the fuse. From the dining room,
Mother yelled, *"Daddy, no!"* Then the battlefield rumbled
under my feet. My head thundered. Smoke drifted over
the tombstones. Daddy laughed. And I thought: When the first
drunken Pilgrim dragged out the cannon at the first Thanksgiving—
that's when the Indians left.

from *Earth's Mirror*

8. *Two Girls*

That day I reached and swept the flies from the face of a
Vietnamese girl on the bed of a pickup truck, until I realized she
was dead and stopped, is the day I will never forget. Of all days,
that is the day.

They crowded her eyes, until her eyes were as black and swirling
and indecipherable as the eyes of Edvard Munch's *Madonna*.

When I backed off, the whirlpool revealed such beauty my spine
melted. Such beauty I thought I couldn't live another moment.
Such beauty my soul dissolved. My heart died and revived, died
and revived, died and revived.

This pariah walks the streets remembering a girl. This one
understands death's dimensions. This one dreams of a corpse
without morbidity.

She comes to me in dreams, and at moments in the street after
work, at five o'clock, in that ecstatic period before the fish
markets close, and in my bed at night, where she still lives, as
alive as the one who lies beside you.

9. *Still life*

There you lie. Nothing a man of my qualities could ever say
would track you down. I've spent too many days hustling food
and shelter. My hands are scarred, and my face and voice, from
hard labor and fist work. It was all boring, but all necessary.

By track you down I mean . . . I don't know what I mean. We
search for many things at once. Right now, I'm searching for a

way to talk a friend out of suicide during late-night phone calls, the static on the line an ocean between us, unable to come up with any reason that makes sense to him, except to say it's selfish, I want him in my life for all my life, and certainly there must be others, to which he says I'm self-indulgent. I'm also trying to understand ancient astronomical planetariums, the way a bird was glaring at me, something my doctor said (while the poor drop dead in the streets for lack of pills), trying to understand why a neighbor is pacing the street, a girl with a gun I saw, how the government gets away with it, a few words of Hopi, Maya glyphs, private armies afraid of the poor, the names of all trees in California, the birds and flowers, shrubs and rocks, the tribes, the weather signs, all the night sky that's visible through waste lighting, the stock market because it's connected to the real government, health insurance because it's connected to the real government, computers because they swerve and crash their promise into the same wall as drugged somnambulist television, why the lights of a city across the bay glitter (it has to do with the flutter of pollution and heavy air), why everyone doesn't just shut off all the lights in the world for one night so we can all see the stars at once for once (it has to do with people sticking guns in your face, I know but don't care—we have all these guns because we can't see the sky and don't know where we are), and I'm harassed by people who just don't get it but won't shut up.

There you lie. Your arms perfect for battle and sleep. Eyes closed, watching something I'll never see. Relaxed as I can never relax. Your nipples hard for some reason. Even if you were purple, the morning light, which I have not slept waiting for, would make you gray. Your mouth open and volcanic. I will never track you down, but I'll search my ignorance, carry my puzzles as if they're profound, walk into rooms and look at things, die slowly, go insane and really try to come home.

Ruby, My Dear

Swept to the bank of the Ganges,
what seemed to be charred wood
were flies clustering a child.

A sin to push it in the water?
I wasn't sure, and left the face
to its slow dissolve. It took hours

walking home, dust darkening
my feet to the sandals' leather.
Perhaps the mynah birds would tug

long enough at the tattered wrap
to thread their nests with cotton.
Ruby, what would you have said to me,

that it was the child's choice?
That sounds like you, purple shadow
under your eyes like the stretch of beach

where we'd walk, low tide reflecting
bracelets, crescent shell earrings
and your necklace of lapis moons.

Didn't you once say *We choose our lives?*
If you were here in Benares you'd turn on
Thelonious with Hawkins on tenor—

This is for me, you used to say
as though Monk was your friend—
then close your eyes,

open them, look into mine:
The grief you feel is only
your own. You got away

with lines like those, sent me
on the dirt path home, crickets
making the sound of stars.

On August afternoons, you'd lay on
the horn of your red "Cropduster,"
tell me it was time to cruise

the shoreline, for cool salt air,
Monk improvising in the back seat.
I'm going to steal you from your father,

you'd tell me, *but you can call him*
from Tibet. I felt old enough to love
someone your age, though I'm grateful

you knew better, let me off easy.
And I've remembered how you wanted
to be left in the Ganges with Mingus,

but today, clouding the river
with your ashes, I felt only loss
until I smelled in this teak house

your Tarot room, the Celtic cross
that brought you to the North
where the man who sells mutton

mouths your name. Perhaps you know this
and have already taken the child
to a world of sandalwood

while the earth feeds itself.
Do you remember Hawk's huge sound,
trying to guess what tree he played?

It could be any of those outside
my window—ashok, coconut, mango.

Tiger Frame Glasses

The squad was made up of three girls from a school. The girls' names was Debbie, Donna, and Shenay. They was stalwart, steady, and statuesque, always going round not hurting old people or weak boys but helping them. They strolled down Ronald Drive and Cahill Street to Nathalie Avenue to way over to Jefferson Estates, where they could be invited in some Body's house for cookies and where they could automatically spot trouble. Things that needed correcting. A yelling mother. A father that liked to observe things too much. A brother that was in danger of getting left back in school with a bunch of stupids. A sister that didn't have no friends and was going to get murderized by some others and furthermore she thought she was going crazy. For instance. That was at day.

At night they came together and decided Who Should Benefit From Our Good Deeds? They all had Good Hearts. They was all big strong girl students, that did science superbly smart and got into the honor roll just from their math grade. You Know Girls Can Be Boy Smart. The Helper Squad was loved by every Body in Amity-ville. They was a home for girls and boys that had secrets and that needed things corrected. The Helper Squad mothers and fathers wanted the girls to be stupendous.

(That's how I made them in my notebook. Stupendous.)

Their mothers and fathers let them talk about babies and how babies came, just as long as they don't have none of their own. Right now you all just help and do right. We love you just like you are. And don't forget: You are the Ones.

(That's how I made them.)

They had us in a circle of two, all by ourself, them close to where the bus comes, me and Bethi in a circle by ourself, but then they broke it up by telling Bethi that I had called her a slow girl in Mr. di Salvo's class yesterday so then I was an only circle. They told her Come Stand over Here by Us. Bethi looked at me with her mouth hanging open, nothing new. She went over to the back opening of their circle. Then it was just me to make a circle out of one person, waiting for the bus which would surely include more agony. Bethi and I were apart, but together by radar we were waiting to get to Park Avenue Elementary and by radar remembering when my head got massacred in a fusillade of blood by Bibi and Crater and Martha and Bellerina last summer on this very corner. We listened to their ugly brains and their ugly ways. I wanted them like my whole Body was fire.

—I'm going with Charlie to The Back. I am his world.

—What you doing there? No one is suppose to be in The Back.

—None of your fucking business.

—The Back is where the lezzies go. You a homo.

—Teeny, tell your sister she's butt ugly. You cunnylingling.

—What's that mean?

—Look in the mirror.

—No one is suppose to be in The Back. They say that's where girls...

—Look in the mirror.

They would giggle like monsters and it would fill in all the air that I had saved up in my head. I was trying to be self-independent and breathe my own air. My notebook was in my bag with all my stories in it and was my own air. I had learned about Indians in the Nineteenth Century being self-independent, especially when the Frontiersmen had it out with them over all the harms they were causing. The wagon trains moved in a circle and pulled out shotguns under the flaps. The Pioneers suffered. They had a dream. That one day this nation will rise up. The Pioneer People built America because they would not let their dream get stoppled. I learned from Mr. di Salvo that the Indians could be awful quiet, holding in their breath in the shrubberies when ambush was near. The Pioneer People would be sitting in the wagon train with women and children, some who could read and write. But they could not make out the thunder in the ground or the smoke signals from the rocks that said: You was born to sacrifice for this great land.

I do the same in my circle.

Ass. Ass hole. Cunny. Four Eye Fuck. Think You a Brainiac, but You is a fucking Re-Tard. You and Your Fucking Notebook Full of Lies. (Why you have to write lies like that?) You and You Re-Tard

Sister. I'ma Kick Your Goddamn Ass. Like I did Last Summer Remember. You better stay indoors. WITH YOUR NOTEBOOK. Slow Girl will be a Dead Girl. Yeah I'm Looking at You. Four Eye Fuck.

The other girls giggle gigantic giggles. Then Bellerina's sister Gimlet and her girl *friend* Big Susie come by on their way to high school and just stand there, letting the girls look them up and down. Every Body drinks in Gimlet and Big Susie and knows in their heart that they are the rulers, even if no Body is allowed to say what else they are. Bethi is just standing there not doing a thing. Because it wasn't *her* head that got massacred last summer, the braids all torn up, the teeth in shatters. The eyes in a clump. No writing hand at all. All because of the notebook I keep with the stories. Only the girls from the bus stop think it was all about them which it was not. Bethi doesn't know what she is doing there in the girls' circle. I make a note to myself that I will have to explain that to her later on. That and a thousand other things like how to be good friends with the teachers. The ones that can still be outraged and feel for you.

I watch their mouths. I try to listen with my eyes close. I can see Gimlet yanking her sister Bellerina by the hair telling her You Better not be Doing It, then lighting up a cigarette in front of every Body and then passing it to Big Susie who runs her tongue along the cigarette before she takes it in her lips and smiles back at Gimlet. From where I am standing, the girls' mouths move to things that don't make any sense, like Teeny's mouth saying over and over, I want visitor hands of cyclone skirt, I want visitor hands of cyclone skirt. Every Body laughs. Which shrinks my only girl circle. Gimlet looks over in my direction but she don't do anything. Big Susie says, Y'all ain't supposed to play like that. That supposed to be your fren! Only she knows it ain't playing. Something will happen that will get my ass kicked again. The other girl circle wants me in-tense. Gimlet puts her hand in Big Susie's jeans behind pocket and she and her keep on walking to the high school. I hold my breath. We watch till they're a speck. I turn my eyes down. I feel what they want. Out under the new tiger frame glasses I'm wearing there is a world of uncovered things like hands, hair, voices, teeth, windows, behinds, desires.

* * *

(They were the most perfect girls I could think of.)

Debbie, Virgo, her favorite color was red, like the setting sun over the mountains you could see from her bedroom window. She was precise, innocent, shy, perfectionist, of service to others. Solicitous. The time she wanted to go with Donna's brother's best friend but her good virtuous held her down. All the times she got a 100 grade in math class, but she didn't say nothing. She was modesty carnation.

Donna was in love with her brother's best friend. He loved her back although he was secretly more in love with Debbie. But there are some bonds and some promises that are stronger than the Heart Dictation. There is Honor. There is Friendship. There is another Girl Truth.

Donna, Aries, was a grade A student and the most beautiful girl in the school. Sometimes rash, sometimes thorny, but always up front. Everyone wanted to say that Cynthia Wiggins was the most beautiful, but secretly they knew that beauty is not just outwardly. No, what about all that on the inside? And Donna's biggest wish in life was to become a veterinarian and take care of sick injured horses.

At the Divine Confabulation Private School For Girls Donna asked to play a slave in the Thanksgiving Assembly in the fifth grade. Everyone wanted to be a Mistress on a plantation, but Donna knew right from wrong. She was her mother and father pride and joy. Her favorite colors was brown and white.

In school Mr. di Salvo asks me if I can spell the word "appreciate." If I can spell it correctly, I will get to be one of the Women in the Pioneer play. I will get to sing "This Land Is Your Land" with the other Women. I will get to have Mrs. Shea from third grade sew me a bonnet and a long apron to wear over my clothes when I walk along the stage with the others. All this for "appreciate" on our weekly spelling bee. Bellerina sees that I am having trouble. She and I are at the middle desk. She has not had her hair straightened in days. There are all these little nubs down the back of her neck. The Ultra-Sheen grease that her mother told her to put in missed her hair and smacks down her neck and shows my reflection in it. I can almost see my corduroy pants on her neck through my tiger frame glasses that everyone makes fun of and calls me F.E.F. cause they know I won't do nothing. I only have one pair of pants. My parents say that we are poor, but not to go out broadcasting that information. How can I help it? My knees are rundown. Every Body knows. And I can't do nothing. But the school bus on page 2 of the spelling book honks to me: *appreciate, appreciate.* The Boloney Butcher for B whispers, I *appreciate* a truly smart girl like you. I am going stark raving for a girl in the fifth grade who is going to get it later on from the girls at the bus stop. A whole bunch of dreams. I want to do something. Will my parents finally go away with us on vacation to the mountains or the seaside like they promised? Will they send me and Bethi to private school—where we *really* belong? A truly smart girl. My brain remembers the melody lane from the day before in the backyard: Daddy mowing the dried-up lawn and whistling "California Dreamer" and Mom singing the commercial for Eight O'Clock Coffee and Bethi trying to get all the words to "Shakeit Shakeit Shakeit" in one line, like there are no other words to the whole song. Me sitting in the bushes with my notebook which is the dream weevil and trying to get it all down the way I would truly like it to happen and looking up in the sunlight and wishing I had a real mother and a real father and a real sister that wanted the utmost best for me, who realized all the dynamite I have in me, like a princess or a very smart and beautiful princess/girl/student. I listen. I want to shout to Bethi, —We're going to the country, We're going to the fair, as those are the other words, but she is really too slow to get anything. I hate her.

Bellerina whispers in my ear, —A-P-P-R-E-S-H-E-A-T-E. I repeat her words. I want to stand in the girls' circle. When I *used to* be there, Bellerina used to play the funniest jokes on me, and I wouldn't get mad. She had told Bibi in secret exactly *where* it would hurt the most on my Body to hit me, and she was right. She stold my notebook to see the stories I wrote in it so she could give the others more ammunition. She informed me that she would get her older brother Beanie from prison to take me to The Back and feel my nubs under my dress. She did all this and still. I want to stand in the girls' circle. I will spin Bethi out, cause she really don't know what it means, the circle. She don't know that I should have what she has, only she don't recognize that for her genuine slowness.

Mr. di Salvo announces that I will be one of the people pulling the wagon across the prairie. They had those, too, you know, when the horses died, and the cattle broke down. I don't have to wear a dress if I don't want to. The girls wearing aprons and bonnets will have to wear a dress under. But I can wear whatever I want to, even my gym suit, as a puller.

The songs I will have to sing with the chorus are "Fifty Miles on the Erie Canal," "Sweet Betsy from Pike," "Carry My Back to Ole Virginny." I will have to walk slow like they did in the old days. They did not run across the prairie. I will have to learn my songs good. Bellerina holds her big teeth under her big hand. She will get to be a Pioneer Woman. She will get a bonnet and an apron. She will get to sit in the wagon while the boys and some unlucky girls pull it. Even though she weighs as much as a ninth grader, one ton, and she is butt ugly.

The teacher is not expecting nothing. I was born on Easter, an Aries baby, so that makes me the kind that is innocent yet secretly commanding. I raise my hand and I get up slowly out my desk. My palms are sweaty. My long braids that I hate for my mother to make on me are messed up already because I've been putting my head down on my boring speller too much. I get up. The gray venetian blinds on the big window hold back the sun with their straight arms and tell me that I am in the right lane. Go on, Girlie! they cheer. They reach down and pat my head like I'm the faithful dog. The doorframe gets ready to move. The tiles on the floor are shivery with delight. Shakeit Shakeit Shakeit. Shakeit all you can. I open my mouth. —Bellerina Brown is a Fucking Ass. Hole. The class goes wild. Shakeit all you can. Shakeit like a milkshake, and do the best you can. The venetian blinds nod yes you can and the clouds outside fall into the classroom and swirl my brains up in a pudding. Bellerina swings for my stomach, but I land on Mr. di Salvo's desk, where I hide with the other butterflies under the stack of math tests from last Wednesday. A staunch stunning wind from the spelling lists stampedes the stalactites on my hands. Bellerina punches but I am too fast. I'm always out her way.

With both eyes open under my tiger frame glasses I see the pretty *one hundred* girls who are in shock and who don't want to consider me anymore for them. The rough *zero* girls have questions for me later: *We ain't know you was like us, Glory!* The snaggle-tooth boys cheer Hip Hip, and BooBoo claps me on the back.

Mr. di Salvo takes me and Bellerina out the play. We will have to sit in Mrs. Shea's class with the third graders while the assembly is on. We will have to write out the words to "The Star-Spangled Banner" ten times and maybe get locked in the closet, which is Mrs. Shea's specialty.

Bellerina looks me up and down. —Later. Today. After School. Your Ass is Grass.

I sit back in my seat. The pencil groove on my desk smiles and asks me, Now that wasn't so hard, was it?

(The story goes on.)

Shenay is a Scorpio. She do not bother with boys at all. She is sexy, strategic, and silent. She figures things out. Shenay has one mission on her mind: Find those who need help, and send in the Helper Squad. That would be her, Donna, and Debbie. They all live on the same street, and at night they are all dedicated to saving.

Shenay can open her bedroom window and get the feel of the ocean waves crashing against the rock. She teaches Donna and Debbie. She tells them to look behind what you see. Look for the genuine-ality of a thing. Donna and Debbie say I don't get it. Shenay says, "Let me give you an example."

When she is lying in her bed at night, she sees gypsy moths fist-fighting in the wall and hears pumpernickel swans discussing yesterday's math problems together. Did you get this one? Sure. That one was a cinch. The swans kiss her on the forehead. Honey, you ain't never told me you were such a smartie.

Shenay says, "Look."

On my way to the principal's office to get my punishment okayed I pass Bethi's classroom and wave to the teacher, Mr. Flegenheimer. Can she come out right now? I just got an important message from our mother and I just want to tell her it in the hall, Mr. Fleg. Private. It's important from our mother.

Mr. Flegenheimer brings Bethi out because he is getting too many complaints from the parents of Special Ed that he is not treating their kids like regular human beings. That he is holding back their bathroom and making them pee in their chairs and sit in it for a long time before calling the nurse and the janitor. That he is closing the venetian blinds and making them sit there, just

like that, so he can put his head down on the desk. Mr. Flegen-
heimer is trying to look different now, but we all know.

—You can talk for three minutes, and I mean three minutes,
Glory. I have a good mind to talk to your mother on the phone to
confirm this, Mr. Flegenheimer says. Then he is gone back to the
class that is howling over something. His eyes are closed.

Bethi is afraid to look at me. She just got allowed into the back
of their circle this morning. She is afraid of what I will do to her.
—Don't worry about that till later, I assure her. I will get you back
later. Right now I want you to do me a favor. I want you to go to
Mr. di Salvo's classroom and tell him to send Bellerina to your
classroom, Mr. Flegenheimer's orders. Can you do that? Okay,
Bethi? Can you do that? I whisper all this to her, but it takes a real
long time before she gets the directions straight. She is not a
retard. She is just slow. Her whole classroom is full of slow kids,
so she don't feel so alone. They get beat up all the time, except for
the large ones that are truly brainless and that can kill you just by
looking your way.

Bethi goes to my classroom and gets Bellerina who calls her
Stupid Ass and Brick Brain all the way back to Mr. Flegenheimer's
door. I'm waiting there. Martha Madison suddenly appears out of
nowhere humming her group of Women's song for Assembly,
"I'se Gwine Back to Dixie." She says in my direction, —You
Gonna Wish You Was Dead Meat. Martha is cross-eyed so she
sometimes scares me and she sometimes doesn't. Now I am only
thinking of my plan. Bellerina slaps her five and then Martha
books. Bellerina turns and looks me dead in the eye. There, I am
there. Shakeit Shakeit.

*The door opened to show the first victim in need: old Mrs.
Goodwin, a faithful soul who had a heart of gold. She was a white
lady who trusted everyone. She lived all by herself in the black
neighborhood of Tar Hill where people live in apartments instead of
normal houses. She can make you believe in mankind all over
again. Hallelujah for Mrs. Goodwin!*

*She had fell down her apartment steps and all the food stamp
cans of food in her grocery bag rolled into the alleyway where Joe the
town bum was laying. "Help me, Joe!" she cried, but he only cried
back, "Mrs. Goodwin, indeed I wish I could! I myself am too weak*

to do much of anything." So they both agonized in tribulations until around the corner came—the Helper Squad!

Debbie helped the old bitty to her feet, but when she found that Mrs. Goodwin couldn't walk, she carried her in her girl arms up the steps to her house and put her in the bed. Donna said, "Debbie, how come you got so strong?" Debbie didn't want to say. Modesty carnation.

Donna placed all the cans of food in their cabinets and to top it off, she cooked Mrs. Goodwin a whole dinner. Saucy Frank Supper with corn and tomatoes in it. Mrs. Goodwin closed her wrinkly eyes with tears of joy. "What would this world be without girls like you?" Donna shaked her beautiful hair and made Mrs. Goodwin feel better just by looking at her.

Meanwhile Shenay was in the alleyway helping Joe the bum to his feet. He smelled strange and warm. She was telling him, "See, if you believe in yourself, you can do it." Joe said he had never believed in himself before today. He was going downtown to get a job at the local school, doing anything. He wants to better himself. Maybe he can raise to a janitor. Shenay, you are a gold mind. Let me thank you.

"Don't thank me. Thank the Helper Squad. We want the world to be the place where you can dream and come true."

"I NEED to thank you, Shenay."

"I said DON'T, old man."

Back then. The daylights whipped out of me. I said I couldn't take it no more. I felt a rippliness in my head from the punches and slides. I told them that I would never tell on them and besides my family has a pool table in our basement. Come over and use it any time. We just don't have some things that go with it. I'll never tell on you. Come over any time. But my head was getting pulverized, and in reality I was already on a cloud floating up to the sky. The voices around said, You ain't got no pool table. Your family is poor as dirt. Don't you go on putting on airs. My lips realized, How did you know that word: *airs*? Then my head got completely mashed up. Meanwhile Beanie, Bellerina's brother, waved to me from his car and laughed because it was truly funny seeing the smart-ass skinny one with the spy notebook of no-good gossip bout everyone on this block get the daylights whipped out of her and maybe he even saw what I wrote about a guy like him in my notebook about how strong and handsome but feeling up ladies now what a shame and why do they have to do that when all they have to do is ask and surely someone will say, Yes please.

Bibi and Martha had my head in a lock, and then Crater had the stupendous idea of putting me between the cinder blocks to see if they could make a girl sandwich. Bellerina said, It hurts the most when something hard is lying on top of your moist spot. The other girls looked at her funny. *Where the heck is that?* Bellerina turned her head away. She said into the wind, Why am I the only one who ever knows anything?

It did not get that far. They slabbed me on a cinder block and I felt the blood bath behind my braided head go into my braided eyes and the true way Beanie's snout nose looked came clear in my mind. Spread out like a father's but he was only a guy. Even with that snout nose I saw through to Beanie's handsomeness. Didn't I say so in my notebook? Next to the made-up stories about Debbie, Donna, and Shenay there was this gorgeous guy named B. who went to prison but who was really too fine to really do anything prisonable. He was in secret a millionaire and he was going fix a deserving girl up in private school where they learn and he would be driving a Fifth Avenue. Only in real life now his car says Dodge. He is handsomely driving a Dodge, Away. I felt like laughing and then the blood trinkled to the line that was my mouth, all the way into my neck, later my eyelids. The blood burned deeper the spot of lonely that was already there. We have a pool table. Only problem is we don't have the balls that go with it. Where is every Body running? Why are you going? Wait. But it was too late. I was there half a sandwich for a pillow and no way in hell Beanie in his Dodge was going to give me another look now.

At the bus stop I am always shrinking of the girls. Fall Spring Morning Bedtime School Clothes PJs. I want to be with them but I am also shrinking. I wish I was dumber. I wish I was getting left back. I wish I weighed a hundred twenty pounds in the fifth grade. Then I would be in the bus stop circle. I could stop feeling Bethi breathe down my plaid dress in her waiting. She stands so close. I need to do something to her, even though she will never tell on me, and that fact makes it more stupider to do it in the first place.

My mother thinks that I am incomprehensible for wishing these kinds of things. To be left back and big. My father just laughs in the background, while he is watching *Sixty Minutes*. He laughs, Just one look at Glory's math grades and you can tell she's gonna be in the fifth grade a long time, maybe years. I would've got a horse whipping. You don't know how easy things are nowadays. It's the state of cultural illiteracy. Then he goes back to watching. Mother adds, And another thing: You better stop bringing up private school, girl. It's just incomprehensible. Do you think we made out of money? Then Father adds, And you better stop writing in that damn notebook and write something for Mr. di Salvo that will get you passed into sixth grade. Bethi smiles at me but I don't want it. Then they go on. Mother is folding clothes and telling Bethi what to put down on her spelling worksheet and my father is saying to the TV, —I Been Told You That Last Year, Stupid Ass, and I am doing nothing important, just standing there in an invisible cloud of butterflies, roaches, and wasps, all asking me to be their best friend.

Bellerina looks me up and down in the hallway. —What you doing here?

Before I can open my mouth she says, —You want me to permanently damage that shit-ass face of yours?

—Bellerina, let's you and me go to The Back. No one will know.

—Now what in Shit's Heaven do I want to go to The Back with you for? You ain't no Body. Forget it. I'ma kill you.

—Aww no, Bellerina, I have something really big to tell you out there. If you know this you will be Boss of the Girls. You will have the Power.

—What in Shit's Heaven?

—Please come with me. Then you can whip my ass in front of the whole school. Let's run to The Back. Okay? Let's run. Let's run.

Debbie ran across little Tiffany Hammond. Tiffany was in tears, and her brown curls glittered in the sun. "What is the matter, dear child?" Debbie asked. Tiffany said it was all these words she couldn't get on her spelling quiz. She was going to fail third grade. She couldn't even make up a spelling story. She sat on the steps of her apartment and wept perfoundly. Debbie put her arms around Tiffany.

"Let me help you," she said. By magic, Donna came with Shenay. The two of them explained spelling tips to little Tiffany. They taught her how to practice to win. Meanwhile Debbie thought of a story that could put together the words Gather Garnish Gaze Gazebo Generous Generosity Genuine Ghost Gibberish. They read Tiffany's story out loud and they laughed in harmony. Tiffany said, "You saved me from impending doom, all you are geniuses," and they laughed when they realized that Genius was a spelling word, too.

Shenay said why don't we start a spelling club at school cause she said girls need to know more spelling words than boys so that they wouldn't be sitting on no steps in the middle of the day crying their goddamn eyes out. "Girls can be strong, Tiffany. Tears ain't always the answer," Shenay said. Donna said that a spelling club would be just fine. Donna said that she had something to discuss with Debbie in private, so goodbye, Shenay. Shenay thought a minute to herself. Then she said, "Yeah, goodbye, Girls."

Bellerina and I snuck out the window over the emergency door. I sent Bethi back to her class, only I didn't know if she could make it without blabbing. Me and Bellerina walked half the way to The Back. We didn't say a word. We looked over by the handball court and saw the High Schoolers smoking there. They cursed all the time but it didn't sound like the way elementary cursed. It came over elementary lips like bowling balls except Bellerina who it was her natural way of life. High Schoolers could curse up a storm and when it was over, you realized that all they said was, Hi, how you doing? Bellerina waved to her sister standing out there with Big Susie but they didn't notice her. Gimlet had her warm arm around Big Susie's shoulder, and their faces was really next to each other. I felt my secret long heart.

Charlie came out the shack that stood in the corner of The Back. We could see him from halfway. Charlie wiped his mouth along the edges with his pointer finger and his thumb. He was big and small at the same time. He waved to us to come. —I'm feeling warm! he shouted. He was leaning against the shack.

Bellerina looked a bit scared. She turned to me. —So what you want? What you got to tell me?

I swallowed. —Bellerina. I don't want to fight anymore. What is it about me you don't like? I can change! My notebook is only stories. Of how things can maybe be. I am really smarter than people think. I can change! BELLERINA!

—I don't like your fucking face. Can you change that?

I also don't like your slobbering Re-Tard sister. Why she have to stand with us?

I also don't like it you think you are better than me. You think you a Brainiac. Well, let me tell you. That's a damn lie. Write that in your damn notebook full of lies. Four Eye Fuck In Liar. You hurt a lot of people with them damn lies. That's what you are.

Bellerina walked away just like that. So my plan had failed. I just kept my head down and my eyes closed. Bellerina walked to the shack. It was a stupid plan when you got right down to it.

I sighed with the future. Your Body never gets used to it. It hurts more each time. I de-test the feeling of hands messing me up. I am a girl made out of brown peel, not iron and steel. I also de-test the eyes. They can mess you in a way that makes you afraid to sleep at night, get up in the morning. The eyes can push you off into a lonely circle, like the circle of me and my sister, like the circle of me. I de-test it all.

Bellerina called back to me, —I'ma get you this afternoon. Me and the girls. You better be ready. Drag me out in the cold. You lucky Charlie is here for me.

She went with Charlie in the shack. Charlie said, —Dag! Dag!, and I saw other High Schoolers fast-walking there. She had said: —I'm his whole world.

Bellerina's sister Gimlet shook her head when she saw Bellerina going in the shack. Big Susie grinned. Gimlet usually doesn't care, even when she swears she will kick anyone's butt who messes with her little sister. She took a puff of cigarillo, down to her feet. She looked and shaked her head. Big Susie laughed, —She's going to get *lit up*.

They were needed again. Little Bobby Lee had fallen off his sister's banana seat bike and was bleeding. Another boy stood near him. "Help!" the big boy cried. Soon a crowd was there. No one was

*capable of doing nothing. Lucky for them Debbie, Donna, and
Shenay was speeding on their way to the place.*

*"What happened?" Debbie asked. The big boy told her. The crowd
agreed. Bobby was so clumsy when you weren't looking. His sister
was in tears.*

*Shenay stepped up and looked at the big boy. She waited a
moment with eyes that didn't move. She said, "I'm waiting." The
crowd growed silent. The sun didn't move from the sky. She said,
"I'll wait." The big boy looked. A river of pee ran down his leg and
he bawled. "It was not all my fault," he bawled.*

*Shenay stepped back. The crowd laughed and started smacking
the big boy upside his head. Someone held little Bobby Lee in their
arms and rocked him to sleep like a scared hummingbird. Shenay
stepped back until she was just a speck on the distance.*

I sat down on the steps of the handball court, and out the
stretch of my eye, I could see the shack at The Back. High School-
ers went in and they stayed. The sky hung blue. Gimlet walked
over to me out of nowhere. I had to catch my breathing. I was
thinking about burning my notebook. It was just a bunch of sto-
ries. A fire would prove something. Or I could take cinder blocks
and make a sandwich. That would be better proof.

Gimlet stopped in front of me and said she heard I was going to
get my ass kicked. That's what she heard. She looked over at the
shack. She shrugged her shoulders. But then she just kept on
walking, like the air was not holding her down.

*Shenay called a special meeting. It was at her family's ski lodge,
and her parents were both away on a medical mission in the Heart
of Africa. "I want to speak to you both from my soul," she explained
the girls.*

*She pulled Darnell Williams out her closet. "Is this the boy you
two been dreaming about?" The girls nodded yes. "Well, stop it right
now. We have a large mission at hand. What will happen if we don't
save things?" The two others didn't have anything to say in their
shame. "What will happen if we ain't responsible for the lips and
knees and heads and hearts of others?"*

*Shenay took Darnell Williams and kissed his mouth into her own.
She put his face on her chest and said, "There. Ooh there." She told*

him, "Also: Kissing me on my neck drives me wild. Now you going to have to give me what you been giving these two." There was no arguing with Shenay.

The other two said, "We understand," and went on home to do their social studies homework. They realized that Shenay could have it all, but she was doing this to be responsible. She taught them a uplifting lesson about girls in the life of the world.

In the corner of my eye I saw Bellerina fast-walk out of the shack in The Back. She was saying something but then Charlie pulled her back in. Her shirt was open. I could see the sides of it blowing in the wind. I could see that she was not wearing a undershirt but a womanly brassiere. She had meaty sides.

In the hallway Gimlet was talking to the Principal Blackburn. Big Susie was nodding yes to everything. Gimlet cried, —And if my goddamn sister can't be learning here in school I'ma go to the damn Super-in-ten-den to get some answers. You suppose to be watching over these kids. And they hanging all over the place who knows where doing shit.

Principal Blackburn said, —Gimlet, it's good that you watch out for Bellerina. She's been having trouble. Why hasn't your mother called? Or your father? We need your parents to take action.

—I'm her parent. Shit. I'm just as good.

—This is really the job of a father, Gimlet. You are pretty young yourself. Please send your father in to see me.

—You see Big Susie? Well, she is Bellerina's father, if I say so. Get that through your thick head, Mrs. Blackburn. Shit.

Shenay pushed Darnell Williams out a five-story window. His Body was a blood bath. She didn't have time for that kind of mess. She knew there was more important things in life besides girls loving boys. Why do girls always be helping others? Why don't girls grow up to be mad scientists? Why don't girls grow up and love other girls and fight over them instead of boys? The world had too many fences in it for Shenay. She called the ambulance to come and pick up the blood bath.

Mr. di Salvo came outside and grabbed my shoulder. Bethi was next to him, looking guilty in her slow way. She knew I was going to fix her. Mr. di Salvo asked, —What the hell are you doing out here? pulling me back into Park Avenue. He dragged me past Gimlet and Mrs. Blackburn. Mr. di Salvo listened and took out his hanky and wiped the sweat off his lip. —Hell, he said.

He turned to me. —You are lucky your sister blabbed. You trying to get your butt beat? Always looking for a way out of math. You barely passed the test from last Wednesday. But just how would you know that, Glory? You just sitting out here enjoying the day when the rest of us are looking over the math answers. You. You. You. You. You.

I looked at my sister before we dumped her off at Mr. Flegenheimer's. I could not think of any big evil to scare her with. She blinked at me. I growled, —What you want, Bethi? Stop wasting my precious time. Stop looking at me. Wipe your nose. Close your damn mouth.

But Bethi put her nose close to my shoulder. She sniffed me. She whispered so only I could hear, —I don't want you get beat up, Glory. I going to help you. We going to poison them. We going to kill them so we can stand back together. I want to be with you. We going to make poison.

I stopped. I hugged my sister. I didn't care. I hugged her till we got to Mr. Flegenheimer's, where the kids were screaming like gorillas from behind the door. Mr. di Salvo made me let her go.

Shenay didn't let her mind go down, like some other girls she knew. She concentrated. When she saw a girl, she did not try to explain it that the wind or the stars or the pencils told her to do it. She did not have to go crazy in her head to feel the genuine things. She walked up to the girl and held her in her arms and said, "You are my present to me." That's all there was to it. She would always help Those In Need, Shenay would. She did not have to be a nut case.

Big Susie saw me and walked next to me on the way back to Mr. di Salvo's class. Mr. di Salvo held my arm tight. He was thinking about how I had been a different girl. That meant *zero* girls' punishment. But by the time we got to our classroom, Mr. di Salvo was thinking of letting me be in the chorus to sing one of the assembly songs. He said I would have to learn the words and not just goof off with my head in the clouds like I am prone to do. Could I learn the words and not be a screwball. Mr. di Salvo was feeling for me and that was a good surprise.

Big Susie was walking next to me. She leaned over and her chest touched me on the shoulder. She whispered in my ear that I was not getting beat up that day or on any day. Bellerina was not going to get me. Bellerina was not going to get anyone. Big Susie touched my hair with her hand. She said, —You girls are scared shitless. Then you go and do some shit. Just wait. And then Big Susie was gone.

> *I'se going back to Dixie*
> *No More I'se gwine back to wander,*
> *My Heart's Turned Back to Dixie*
> *I can't stay here no longer*
> *I miss de old plantation, my friends and my relation,*
> *My heart's turned back to Dixie, and I must go.*
>
> *I've hoed in fields of cotton*
> *I've worked up on de river*
> *I used to think if I got off*
> *I'd go back there, no never*
> *But time has changed de ole man, His head is bending low*
> *His heart's turned back to Dixie, and I must go.*

I sat in the desk in the back of the room, next to Martha Madison. She tried to look rough and scare me into last year, but I kept my eyes right on her till she looked away. The venetian blinds asked me how I felt. The pencil groove in my desk wanted to know why I wasn't talking to it anymore. I said out loud, —I don't want you. *No more.* Martha Madison winked her eyes in the other direction trying to do like I was crazy. Only I wasn't.

You can change things just by ignoring the furniture. You can get your own kind of strength. I looked hard at Martha Madison. From the side, her eyelids had on a trace of her mother's eye makeup, Blue Oceans. Martha always stole her mother's makeup to come to school in. She had dreams. The desk wood was silent. The venetian blinds were just venetian blinds. I looked hard at Martha. I also had dreams. I will keep my notebook in my school bag. That's the proof. I will get back in that circle.

Ragcutters' Heaven

on the art of William H. Johnson

1. Florence, South Carolina—1915

Harlem she said
or he thought she said
she and every other hotel in town.
Stopped dead on the wooden walk
outside her white
porte-cochère
he watched the red sun roll
into her rooftops.
She said *Harlem*   or was it the bark
of steam from a black
railroad workhorse breaking up
and joining partners like some
Dancemaster with a plan in his head:
You—Charleston
no you—north to Wilmington
all evening slide and turnabout
to a steel motif.

You listen to me
William Henry Johnson
firstborn living son of Alice and Henry Johnson
cleverest child at the Wilson School for Colored:
I am sinking into the earth
these spit-shine polished
floorboards fuel for a bone fire.
Give it fifteen and you won't even
know me at first.
Then you'll turn all energetic
and paint me drunk
crazy on the arms of creaky trees
buckled under the weight

of this wheel you'll fly close to
in every sky but mine.

Jacobia said *Go on now go*
but he was already gone
to where Uncle William prepared
a cot for him in Harlem
and even then she would not stop talking no:
Remember this day when I
am what they want when
the smoker puffs in from Florida
my double-deck porches
pushing out to meet them.
Paint me my red front door—
not a day in your life you could walk
through it and order a drink
of cool water so move on boy
before this whole town settles
in your lap for our own sweet reasons.

II. Provincetown—1924

Nothing like this morning,
when it hit that sweet spot.
White friends in white clothes sang out
the score the grass still fresh
on the court you mowed yesterday.
When the girl ask you *What country*
are you from anyway?
there's something to be said for silence
that silence is not saying.

Silence is back in a railroad town
setting pins at the bowling alley.
Silence totes palette and paints
for Hawthorne's Open-Air Life.
Doesn't the sun exaggerate

herself all for silence?
Nothing like this morning
when she bloomed on canvas.

III. Cagnes-sur-Mer—1928

The sun is your father you paint Him red
the first and last color in Creation.
He makes you to lay down your life
and you do. He leads you cross oceans
cross rivers. Cross glaciers
that burn your knees you follow
your daddy's trail till one morning
you greet Him like any old star
you say oh honey why are You lying there
and carry Him home a burning
bush on your shoulder.

Mother tacks a scrap of yellow cloth
above the earth forever. She shows you how
to squeeze and wring Her wrinkled
rags. You nod all right all right I get it.
You hear the thump of the iron
watch Her steam and press the acres out.
She says open your hand to the sun
flatten your body out in the field.
She lets you do it: draw and stitch
together the ripped Word.

If you take the sun as your wife
She will someday turn cool as midnight.
All summer She rolls her white body
smearing her scent from peak to peak.
You can try all manner of things: rock Her
in your two arms the way she likes it
talk to her all night. She is not able to stop.
Where the Spirit urged there the Wheel went

and the noise was like rushing water.
Even the sun will break up—
already its seeds blow to the islands.

IV. *Kerteminde, Denmark—1931*

—Oh Mama it's enough
to make a smart man cry
the way you can sit there
easy as breath unweaving
all your daywork.

Maybe I stood at the door
rolled in a Brother's blanket—
herring and vomit—Woman please
come warm me clean through.
She says *Wait a minute Willie won't you?*

—*There,* she says.
She worries out the flaw. —*That's ten o'clock
when the wind picked up and I thought
of my husband the painter
out fishing with the men's folk.*

This loom of hers can't walk.
Evenings I anchor with my pipe
watch her beat the stripes out of hiding.
Watch her send the shuttle flying
through layers of colored warp.

Watch her stop herself   winding
the raveled thread back to the breast
beam. You think she numbers
her days the way we do? She spends her hours
like centuries like hours.

I wrote things I shouldn't have
to those Harlem connoisseurs.

No way now to throw it back.
Like I told Brother T—
"Never going catching herring again!"
He laughed at my Danish and sent me home.

v. *Harlem—1939*

It's the mule's day off and the sun's night out.
Blue houses dip their stilts in the cool tide.
Chartreuse babies sprout from charred stumps
of wannabe-trees-again. *Wave at the*
planets, Child. Women, lift your hands
and kick your frowns off. Jesus
is a blues man, keeps repeating himself.

He sings, You got to.
He sings, You got to believe.
Sings you got to believe I said
not half the man said I said.
We vote for Him with our shoes.
We vote to get born, no turning back. Regret
is a burlap blanket saved for rainier days.

vi. *Self-Portrait in Three Positions—New York, 1944*

> *"I am still at my shipyard, painting, doing my own work—*
> *all good art I'm doing now, thanks to my Radio."*

Come on in. Mind the water now mind the wind
and most of all that last
step. Come on over
where the light's still good.
We want you to meet
our brother
for he is the best   as far as men go
all the better to deal with life's
affronteries.
We have dressed him in white

87

to honor the desert sun.
Note how like the sun—
his panoramic gaze
and his wife dead just
yesterday.

Is it morning yet?
Stand here why don't you.
But watch out for the mountain
stone-cold and waiting
for an avalanche.
It has been—we were just
remarking—
how long *has* it been
since he had anyone to chat to
concerning aesthetics?

Next to him
are we not clowns in striped shirts?
Next to him are we not chaff
blown across the world
and food for swine? Him
he's spent his penny
in this one wise room
taking direction. Sit
down I said. Is that
morning? And who
gave you permission
to turn that radio down?

Listen. He is not asking for much.
He does not eat
much. But please
take a little something
yourself. As for us we are
older and broke down
some time ago—Hell—if we could
drink we'd make a highball

of a Harlem moon.
Could eat we'd eat a Nazi.
Could paint   oh to paint again
wouldn't we pack this brother back
to where he came from?

Note: Quotations of Johnson in Parts IV and VI are from Richard Powell's Homecoming: The Art & Life of William H. Johnson *(Washington, D.C.: Smithsonian Institute, 1991).*

Waiting to Wake Up Française

After Kirs in tall glasses at the Café Dupon,
we roamed the cobblestone streets, each
storefront window a stage, empty save for its props
and the dark behind them. A *boulangerie*
every block, five blocks to the bus stop.
He'd persuade me to drive in his Peugeot,
a silver compact stick shift. Angers at night,
a spotless ghetto of thin white buildings,
no midnight, no field there, billboards
unfamiliar with the frenzy of circumflexes
and *accents graves.* The car left running
at my door, Vincent's hand suddenly at the small
of my back, my knee knocking the gear shift,
his throat choking something trite but
passionate, *"Tu me craques,"* a matchstick
flaring, far-off tires squealing, our faces gone blue
under the streetlamp. No familiarity
even in the way lip pressed
lip, I decided to be untouchable, never
to drag my fingers down the back of a man's
shaved neck. Nor to speak of what blackened
like numbers on the oval license plate's
fine glitter. The town, whose markets sold
flowers and used paperbacks of Proust,
turned frightening, the American films
became oddities I refused to see, denied them
like Peter. Outside nameless cafés
crowded with canvas umbrellas, I sat holding
a café noir too bitter to drink.
Sugar cube balanced at the rim of the cup,

I watched the dark bleed through
until it crumbled. I read Irish poetry,
curled pages of a journal pressing too hard
as I wrote, words half-French, half-American.
In bed, I contemplated defenestration,
laughter, abuse. I turned each away.

ALEXANDER GUREVICH

Komi

translated by Phil Metres

This drilling rig lies in the forest tundra.
One rises on command, sleeps ears cocked,
and waits for the cry "All hands on deck!"
at an untimely hour, mindless of the weather.
It snows here—but it's summer in the States,
and I'm free to conceive in futile ways
what you eat and wear, who are your friends
(I'm convinced that everything's in its place).
For the charter flight is like a rendezvous:
while it bends around the globe toward you
this eight-legged, tiny center of the universe
spins a web of speech over space.
For the best of all personal trips, Norka,
is when one pays a tariff to oneself in time:
you see, knowing you're now a real New Yorker
is worth it, at least for the sake of the rhyme.
Well, I didn't start drinking or scandalize the home,
didn't quit my job or leave my family:
only left awhile for the Republic of Komi,
where it takes a day's flight to return to them
and still more to reach you, and more, to life.
If, not putting myself above the latter—
if I could pass the exam at the best school,
if I knew—oh, Norka, if I knew better,
I'd stay now amidst human beings, not mosses,
wouldn't tremble in September with this dry frost.
But since I've started talking to you in poems,
I can't return to that shameful old prose.

* * *

With this new wave music in my ears
and sitting in the well-heated cab of a Ford,
I observe, like a guest from a foreign land,
stacks of frozen timber, all second sort,
sheepskin coat, bare neck, end of a gun's barrel,
ear-flapped cap—on a tower, above barbed wires;
and the road is lifeless and smoothly white,
and two pieces of ice shine in the soldier's eyes.
The passes are checked, the gesture made,
and the car skids a little on ice when driving
into what my Americans call the gulag:
the abbreviation unknown to them, alien.
And the major of the internal troops
in his office shakes hands with everyone round,
while the scenes stuck in your head come forth:
descriptions of death, scurvied gums and stench.
And while you try to polish with English gloss
the militiaman's words about selling logs—yes,
it's like silently switching the wave of your brain
from the language of terror to the slang of progress.
But the major, alas, has no time for deals:
he's in a hurry and worried for his career,
for a convict's been run over by a tractor;
everything's postponed till the case is clear.
So we leave. And our wheel-track, just laid,
is already concealed by a layer of new snow;
there are fir trees and bushes along the way,
and I do exist in the world, feel life's cost grow,
and it's all to my liking—the blizzard, the frost
and the driver, as versatile as a fox.
"A gulag's a gulag," our boss says in English to me
—indeed, it's difficult not to agree.

* * *

From the Cosmos Inn in Pechora, Komi,
to the Planet Hotel in Minsk, Belarus,
having flown through space, having found
the room number, knocked and rushed in,
talked all night to your close friend—now
a consultant, an engineer in Bedford,
Massachusetts—and blown to Moscow
in a car, just making it to the airport

and already descending over serene flatness
of the North, its snowy trees and swamps,
you feel ashamed, having failed to learn
the heart is dearer than jobs and wives
and teaches you love for a neighbor,
this wise land reminds you in its northern tongue
how your friend broke his knee skiing
as a child—another life—in Zelenogorsk.

Again, The River

for Geneviève Pastre

Early summer in what I hope is "midlife,"
and the sunlight makes me its own suggestions
when I take my indolence to the river
and breathe the breeze in.

Years, here, seem to blend into one another.
Houseboats, tugs, and barges don't change complexion
drastically (warts, wrinkles) until gestalt-shift
dissolves the difference.

Sentence fragments float on a wave of syntax,
images imprinted in contemplation,
indistinct impressions of conversations
which marked some turning.

Food and drink last night with a friend—we've twelve years
history of Burgundy and good dinners
and as many books off the press between us
toasted together.

Writing is a difficult form of reading.
Paragraphs that roll away from their moorings
seem like passages to another language
half-comprehended.

Sometimes thought is more like a bad translation.
Hazy shapes resistant to sentence-structure
intimate—but what do they mean, exactly?
Texture, sound, odor

(dockside, urinous, up on green slopes, roses
in full bloom like elegant girls of forty)
imprint images in aleatoric
absence of order.

Isolated words can unlock a story:
what you ate, she felt when she heard the music,
what's brought back by one broken leaf, whose sticky
sap on a finger

named a green, free season to city children.
Now, daylight's duration is equinoctial:
spring is turning swiftly to summer; summer's
ripeness brings endings.

I can feel a change in the weather coming.
When I catch a glimpse of myself in mirrors,
I see someone middle-aged, with my mother's
sallow complexion.

Whom do we write books for? Our friends? Our daughters?
Last night's dinner companion has two daughters,
women in their thirties with strong opinions.
My child is younger,

might say there won't be books in the "2000's,"
just "hard copy" "downloaded" from computers.
Children won't haunt library aisles, as I did,
tracking their futures.

(What about the homeless man reading science
fiction on the steps of St. Paul, a tattered
paperback, a galaxy on the cover
he was approaching?)

Houses are precarious or unsettling.
We who left them young, and applaud our daughters'
rootlessness still scrutinize wind-chapped faces
of pavement-dwellers.

"Every woman's one man away from welfare"
—he may be a college trustee, a landlord
or a bland, anonymous civil servant
balancing budgets.

My friend's postcard goddesses, morning teapot,
Greek and Latin lexicons, Mac computer,
fill the magic cave of a room she works in
which she'll be leaving

when her lease is up (as provincial theater
troupes strike sets, pack trunks), lares and penates
ready to be set on a desk and bookshelves
in closer quarters

where she'll reestablish haphazard suppers
on her Cévennes grandmother's round oak table.
Where will I be? Too many airline tickets
away to answer.

(I lead two lives superimposed upon each
other, on two continents, in two cities,
make believe my citizenship is other
than that blue passport's.)

But today there's wind on the Seine; a tugboat
with embroidered curtains and gardened windows
looks like home as it navigates the river
toward other moorings.

Our Town Intermezzo

Gats' tag
              over *Shooters'*
      on *DOAs'*
covering Dog Tony's confession
          DOWN WITH MINE, red
black green
      yellow paint
           shrouding the orange
brick of the *Brews-n-Chews,* first
      wall you see
after Memphis Avenue crosses the God
          of Abraham
off the list of possible
      hallelujahs and falls in love
with the God of Jacob, the one
          you can't look at
      without your eyes going to fire.

* * *

AK, said one doctor. Uzi, the other. In a month,
bandages off, Deena looked at the half-moon
chewed from her shoulder. Outside, Jasmine
and LaTisha and Carly in halters, throwing signs
and sipping Cokes. Deena fingered the rough edge
of absence, watched in the mirror as she traced
a new body, smooth flow of her arm gone,
a distraction from eyes and smile and breasts.
She tried a bandanna, long-sleeve T, worked hard
to fill the mirror with the juice of how she used

to look. When she went out, Jasmine and LaTisha
laughed, said a shark got her, said now she got
a grip for her man. Carly walked her off, in
the alley stared, said please can I touch.

* * *

A Blood Stone Villain pours a slug from a 40
into the ground for Jamal. The dead
    are thirsty, want beer, want food and light

and air if they can get it, when we look
the other way. The crack of 9's
    and 25's waves across the block, a little spice

in the palm, the recoil a tribute, a prayer.
Jamal's brother an OGC, god of time,
    interpreter of the scar, complete with telepathic

skin and 220 stare. He doesn't say anything
as others begin the dirge of revenge,
    offers no prayer to his trembling hands, to the sky's

indifferent blue. He knows the dead refuse to leave,
slip through the throats of needles,
    whisper your name during sex and wear your clothes,

leaving them on the wrong chair. Jamal was hands
and breath and hair, a crooked mouth,
    stupid jokes that went nowhere. As he walks

out of the shop, his brother watches taggers turn Jamal
into history, a black face, blood-red name.
    The song says *Gonna die gonna die make it last*

not first. Jamal's brother makes it to Memphis, sits
on the curb and listens to the sun
    burn leaves and grass, to the sun touch the dirt

and street and cars with equal affection. He's shaking
every wish from his body, each thought
       from his mind, he's saying no again and again

like rain falling from a crippled sky, a fast and violent
chant, as if the body lives inside
       the word, as if by breath this life can be undone.

COLETTE INEZ

Reflections of the Lady Ch'ang

Half-awake she hears hooves at the door—
a stallion enters her Chamber of Longing.
When the door thunders shut

she recalls the fury of her childhood;
Mother's venomous beauty,
Father, adept at lighting amber

in the eye of the sexual god.
The listless husband picked out for her
has left her without heirs.

Beyond that gate the dreaming dog
paws at dragonflies that hover between heaven
and earth. The Lady

in the Hall of the Star that Rewards Long Life
conjures a horse to speed through clouds.
He balks at her command.

She twirls the gold charm sent by a lord
with his ode to a roan mare in autumn.
On tiles thinned by wind, rain, sun,

lie bare prints of her frenzied walk, back and forth.
Forest animals track the night sky.
The reconciliation she struggles to release

is a Leaf Wing pressed from a cocoon,
the cracking of the tortoise through its shell.

In Frost

translated by Khaled Mattawa

I knelt to tie my shoes in the frost
and heard the rattle of an Indian's throat
or maybe the groan of an animal led to slaughter
I imagined men bearing their weapons   extinct
since The Fifth Article of the *Bill of Rights* was recited
since all applauded it and drank a toast to dynamite
as a charm against evils
I could not control myself   I kicked off my shoes
danced and danced with the lightness
of one returning to heaven
until my feet swelled
And as I felt the bed for the remains of memory
the memory of forests   meadows   pavements and streets
the memory of mountain goats and eagles and dinosaurs
pleading with me
to give storms the leap of motion
to give horses the calm sleep
of a veteran of a war of beasts
And as I felt the bed
for the remains of the pain of memory
I saw one of the extinct men—
deep-set eyes and a torch behind them—
point his weapon at me

ALICE JONES

Afterlife

The front door's latch slides into its brass socket,
the kind of sound that pushes you off,
like a flip turn at the pool, your thighs recoil
and you're out past the flags, well on your way...
only I'm talking about the last lap, when there's no
next turn, the future is over, and if you believe in it:
delusion, although you'd love to wake up and
learn you'd been wrong all these years, that
you're not really underground, but are still
precious you, still own your brown eyes
or some ethereal equivalent, blink and find out
you've become a little cove, can still feel
the tides of a larger ocean and respond
as it flushes out the depths of your algaed bay,
wakes up the starfish, tickles the anemones,
one eye open in surprise, that human dream,
turning goodbye into transcendent hello, finding
your small self more indelible than the earth
we've destroyed behind us, this blindness
that won't die, won't say oh yes, I'm one of them,
the swallows who eventually drop from the sky,
or the drought's grass, a breath let out
that won't be sucked in.

For the Love of the Game

Give me a man with a quick first step,
with court vision that takes in all of me,

a man who can play in the paint,
score from all over, finding my perimeter,

a man who can drive my lane.
Give me a man who makes his free throws,

ready to shoot two whenever I demand.
My interior defense isn't tough to crack,

I'm wide open, and I can handle the ball.
I don't care for monster dunks,

for slam-jam-thank-you-ma'am.
I'd rather have a man who can teach me

the delicate technique of the finger-roll,
a man who doesn't bang the boards

but knows how to rebound,
how to come from behind,

an assist leader, a shooter, a penetrator,
a man who knows how to stay out

of foul trouble, hands off
the opposing team's cheerleaders.

I want this madness
to last much longer than March,

to stage endless tournaments
on a court not polished but rumpled,

a sweaty site where the pairings are known,
the brackets full, championships staged

whenever we feel the need for a fast break,
bodies colliding under the basket.

Superstition Mountains, April

We are sitting by a blue lake
in the middle of the desert,
dropping french fries left
from lunch into the mouths
of giant, waiting carp.
You say if this were Poland,
a carp that size would be
a prize for a fisherman
to brag on all his life.
To serve, brown and proud
as any turkey, to his family
on their largest silver plate.

In Iowa, I say, it's against
the law to throw a carp back
once you catch it.
You have to leave it,
gasping, wasted, trashfish
to rot high up on the bank.
All the contradictions—
how in different waters,
fish are not the same.
When we saw each other last,
we thought we'd live forever.
Now you have cancer,
may be dying,
though you are here, alive,
with me today.

So forgive me
if I do not trust tomorrow,
do not want to leave
this unlikely flat blue water

and go back to our hotel.
I want us to keep talking,
our mouths gaping,
eating up our own words,
this desert with its buzzing power lines,
the cactus blooming
pink and yellow flowers
for which we do not have a name.

I want to gobble up
the whole world,
want you to have the time
and appetite to do the same.
Hey, you say, looking down
into a hundred open carp mouths,
do you think they'd eat a pickle?
Never, I say, laughing.
But you drop it, and they do.

Distance

You said she kept leaving you for a dentist, a gay prostitute
whose boyfriend has AIDS, and the short-order cook
who bruised her. She needed someone pretty in her bed.
You'd always wait, stay home until she threw rocks to break
your window, begging to be let in. She taught you to want
bath water so hot you'd lose your senses. You are the one
who loves the most; the woman leaving when her body
heals. One night: gunshots and glass outside, another
woman's bra on the edge of your bed. I ask if you love me.
You wrap me in alpaca, bring me chamomile. *Once a lover,
always a lover,* you say. The following summer, you pack
condoms for your months away, tell me you are afraid
of the space you will come back to. I massage your back
so you can fall asleep. When you are gone, I drink tequila,
receive six letters, four phone calls. *You are the blessing
in my life,* you write. *You are a star.* I stay up, ask myself
if I am a blessing, peel off my clothes for a friend two days
before you come home.

Wisdom

You are blessed in life, she says, touching a match
to a single spicy balsamic leaf, *but if you do not change
your direction, you will end up where you're going.* On her
kitchen counter laboratory, Ah-Pauh simmers sweet oil
from parasitic trees. She asks the thousand-armed goddess
to throw protection over me—small fish my mother wants
to swallow. The hunter hollows a coconut, strung to a tree,
and pushes mango dumplings through the hole,
big enough for a monkey's open hand to slide through.
Too small for his clenched fist to pass. Buddha tells
the woman who carries her dead child on her hip,
*I know a medicine. You will need a handful of mustard
seed from a house where no child, husband, parent, or
servant has died.* The woman walks miles, asking
house to house until there are no more houses. She lays
her child's body in a grove of trees, returns to Buddha.
I have not brought the mustard seed. The living are few.

Elegy for Whatever Had a Pattern in It

1.

Now that the Summer of Love has become the moss of tunnels
And the shadowy mouths of tunnels & all the tunnels lead into
   the city,

I'm going to put the one largely forgotten, swaying figure of
   Ediesto Huerta
Right in front of you so you can watch him swamp fruit

Out of an orchard in the heat of an August afternoon, I'm going
   to let you

Keep your eyes on him as he lifts & swings fifty-pound boxes
   of late
Elberta peaches up to me where I'm standing on a flatbed trailer
   & breathing in
Tractor exhaust so thick it bends the air, bends things seen
   through it

So that they seem to swim through the air.

It is a lousy job, & no one has to do it, & we do it.

We do it so that I can show you even what isn't there,
What's hidden. And signed by Time itself. And set spinning,

And is only a spider, after all, with its net waiting for what falls,
For what flies into it, & ages, & turns gray in a matter of minutes.
   The web
Is nothing's blueprint, bleached by the sun & whitened by it, it's
   what's left

After we've vanished, after we become what falls apart
    when anyone

Touches it, eyelash & collarbone dissolving into air, & time
    touching
The boxes we are wrapped in like gifts & splintering them

Into wood again, at the edge of a wood.

2.

Black Widow is a name no one ever tinkered with or tried
    to change.
If you turn her on her back you can see the blood-red
    hourglass figure

She carries on her belly,

Small as the design of a pirate I saw once on a tab of blotter acid
Before I took half of it, & a friend took the other, & then
    the two of us
Walked down to the empty post office beside the lake to look,

For some reason, at the wanted posters. We liked a little drama
In the ordinary then. Now a spider's enough.

And this one, in the legend she inhabits is famous, &
    the male dies.
She eats its head after the eggs are fertilized.

It's the hourglass on her belly I remember, & the way
    the figure of it,
Figure eight of Time & Infinity, looked like something designed,

Etched or embossed upon the slick undershell, & the way
    there was,
The first time I saw it, a stillness in the pattern that was not
The stillness of the leaves or the stillness of the sky over
    the leaves.

After the male dies she goes off & the eggs

Live in the fraying sail

Of an abandoned web strung up in the corner of a picking box
    or beneath
Some slowly yellowing grape leaf among hundreds of other
Leaves, in autumn, the eggs smaller than the *o* in this typescript

Or a handwritten apostrophe in ink.

What do they represent but emptiness, some gold
    camp settlement
In the Sierras swept clean by smallpox, & wind?

Canal School with its three rooms, its bell & the rope
    you rang it with
And no one there in the empty sunlight, ring & after ring & echo.

The boy who spoke only Spanish read from a book,
Watch him as he used his forefinger to point at each syllable

He would read, read & mispronounce, & stumble over, & go on.

*

And this isn't much of a story either, but it's one I know:

One afternoon in August, two black widow spiders bit
    Ediesto Huerta.
He killed them both & went on working,

Went on swinging the boxes up to me. In a few minutes the sweat
Bathed his face until it glistened, & still he went on working;
And when I asked him to stop he would not & instead

Seemed to begin to dance slowly in the rhythms of the work
Swing & heft & turning back for another box, then

Swing, heft, & turning back again. And within a half hour or so,
Without him resting once but merely swinging box after box

Of peaches up to me in the heat, the fever broke.

3.

In the middle of turning away again, he stopped dancing,
He stopped working. He seemed to be listening to something,
   & then

He passed out & fell flat on his back. It looked as if he had gone
   to sleep
For a moment. I let the idling tractor sputter & die, & by
   the time

I reached him, he had awakened, &, in the next moment, his face

Began twitching, his arms & legs danced to something
   without music
And then stiffened, his jaws clenched & his eyes fluttered open
And turned a pure white. I made a stick from a peach limb
   & tore

The leaves & shoots off it & stuck it between his teeth

As I heard one was supposed to, &, in this way, almost
Killed him by suffocation, & so took his stick out
   & threw it away.

And later lifted him by the one arm he extended to me & pulled
   him up onto
The bed of the trailer. He dangled his legs off the rear of it.

We sat there, saying nothing.

It was so quiet we could hear the birds around us in the trees.

And then he turned to me, &, addressing me in a name as old
    as childhood,
Said, "Hey, cowboy, you wanna cigarette?"

*

In the story, no one can remember whether it was car theft
    or burglary,
But in fact, Ediesto Huerta was tried & convicted of something,
    & so, afterward,
Became motionless & silent in the web spun around him
    by misfortune.

In the penitentiary the lights stay on forever,

Cell after cell after cell, they call their names out, caught in time.

Ring, & after ring, & echo.

In the story, the girl always dies of spider bites,
When in fact she disappeared by breaking into the jagged pieces
    of glass
Littering the roadsides & glinting in the empty light that
    shines there.

4.

All we are is representation, what we appear to be & are,
    & are not,
And representation is all we remember,

Something hesitating & looking back & caught for a moment.

God in the design on a spider's belly, standing for time & infinity,
Looks back, looks back just once, then never again.

We go without a trace, I am thinking. We go & there's
    no one there,

No one to meet us on the long drive lined with orange trees,
Cypresses, the bleaching fronds of palm trees,

And though the town is still there when I return to it, when
    I'm gone
The track is empty beside the station, & the station is
    boarded up,
Boarded over, the town is overgrown with leaves, with weeds

Tall as windowsills, window glass out & dark inside the shops.

The classrooms & school are gone & the bell, & the rope
To ring it with, & the boy reading from the book, forefinger
On a syllable he can't pronounce & stumbles over again & again.

*

All we are is representation, what we are & are not,

Clear & then going dark again, all we are
Is the design or insignia that misrepresents what we are, & stays

Behind, & looks back at us without expression, empty road
    in sunlight
I once drove in a '48 Jimmy truck with three tons of fruit
On it & the flooring beneath the clutch so worn away I could see

The road go past beneath me, the oil flecked light & shadow

Picking up speed. Angel & Johnny Dominguez, Ediesto Huerta,
Jaime Vaca & Coronado Solares, Querido Flacco

5.

And the one called Dead Rat & the one called Camelias;

We go without a trace, I am thinking.

*

Today you were lying in bed, drinking tea, reading
    the newspaper,
A look of concentration on your face, of absorption in some

Story or other.

It looked so peaceful, you reading, the bed, the sunlight over
    everything.

There is a blueprint of something never finished, something
    I'll never
Find my way out of, some web where the light rocks,
    back & forth,
Holding me in a time that's gone, bee at the windowsill
    & the cold

Coming back as it has to, tapping at the glass.

The figure in the hourglass & the body swinging in the rhythm
    of its work.
The body reclining in bed, forgetting what it is, & who.

While the night goes on with its work, the stars & the shapes
    they make,
Cold vein in the leaf & in the wind,

What are we but what we offer up?

Gifts we give, things for oblivion to look at, & puzzle over,
    & set aside,

Oblivion resting his cheek against a child's striped rubber ball
In the photograph I have of him, head on the table & resting
    his cheek
Against the cool surface of the ball, the one that is finished
    spinning, the one

He won't give back.

Oblivion who has my face in the photograph, my cheek resting
Against a child's striped ball.

Oblivion with his blown fires, & empty towns...

Oblivion who would be nothing without us, I am thinking.

6.

As if we're put on the earth to forget the ending, & wander.
And walk alone. And walk in the midst of great crowds,

And never come back.

Night

Because we cannot be together
we live in six notes of Vietnamese
where no one can understand
us except those who speak
in tongues and the language of birds

Because we cannot be together
we boil the root of the telephone cords torn
from the black soils of sleep
hold negatives up to the light
in houses where windows
are yellow eyes, our power
pirated from streetlamps
and flooding gutters

So many years since that chopstick
click of yes, so many years I can count them
in illegal U.S. wars, pueblo feast days,
canceled stamps and blackened wicks

These are the ruined
scripts of what might
have been an ordinary life

These are the monuments

The right to remain

Breathing between the lines

First Things

I am the blue woman
stroking a beaded earring
searching for the right song
at the red light
blue woman, 107 degrees, mesquite
trees fingering the winds
skirts of dust blown
back like Marilyn Monroe
I am the blue woman
wanting a new lipstick
some comprehension of Rwanda
an hour of silence
so cool and moist
melons happen   poems

Time now to feed the fish
lock doors, board a plane
I am the blue woman
who creates life out of
emergency exits, honeyed peanuts
the blue woman waits
the blue woman watches
the blue woman knows
her landing time will be brief.

A Chronicle of the Who & How

apprenticeship

The difference is always road
and you can measure it with rocks or spiders.
The street signs are blue,
the poor lie naked in the parks.
The work of fire never ends
and angels build cities of grass.
Someone will follow a bird to a forest
where child twins are slain.
No king crop here, no fields.
The river swallows the road,
and locusts wrap the sun in gauze.

anatomy of a folk tale

He is ready to follow her.
A song to weep to
when overtaken by dawn
as you lower your gates to a hope
and slide to a paradise of tolerable solitude.
It's midnight now, past spirit and cup.
The traveler is cornered
between privilege and pity,
an echo encased in glass.

a cloud of forgetting

Ice now shields the water
from what cannot be pinned in words.
Does the body still know
that open-mouthed gazing at the world
when hail pocked the copper dust?
I remember weddings and perfumes
and smolders at peace with the palm...

an exile

When I returned
my kin were divided
between dancing and weeping
by the grave. Years passed
and everyone forgot
the false prophet and the horse
that would not leave the sea.
It was easy then to live
on the island (farmers till
their plots). Easy to forget
the waves and their news.

anatomy of an axiom

I have a brother and who else
should I ask for a chronicle
of the who and how.
Far away a man is singing
to a dream, to a fog heavy with wings.
People forget how to die
and each day becomes a porcelain cup.
I kiss the gloss and tread between the heaps.

chapter from a biography

He believed in deception.
The water was an echo
from the womb.
He slept on the cool sand
until strong arms brought him back
to the years. I look at him now,
his briefcase, the girl,
hurried steps on the tarmac
and the waiting days.

memory in a real place

It happened in Tuskegee
when pity delved
to an inexplicable depth,
to a cat and the pungent smell
of her waste, and him standing
at the sink. I was pure
under a fluorescent light reaching
for a thread buried in sand.
My right hand smelled of sandalwood,
my left held a fistful of myrrh.

Mote

He was walking down the highway, Ohio SR 4 between Union City and Butler, singing at the top of his voice. He carried a green plaid suit in a clear plastic garment bag. He did not bother to hitchhike, to actually turn every now and then and lift a thumb. By the city limits sign he had little expectation of catching a ride.

He had been walking for thirty minutes, sweating heavily before he had reached the city limits sign some six miles behind him now. He was free from jail and that was the important news, despite the dust and the sweat and the flies that somehow found him there on the road. At least he was out, out from counting the days. Out from skirting the taunts and near-fights at mealtime, from the deep silences in the cells, those silences he swam through toward sleep. Out, and above all he could float now, his head high and breathing the cool and needful breath of freedom.

Back at the county jail they had returned his original clothes. The suit was a prize won in a tonk game his first afternoon in jail. After his run-in with Late Hit, a man with watery eyes had pushed into his hand a list of job openings around the county.

"Good luck," the man had whispered. Mote's quick scan of the list revealed only a few jobs he qualified for—a cook, stock boy, mill laborer. The folded list rode in his hip pocket now.

Up ahead in Union City a few friends knew him as "The Shark," the one who guarded his territory and sought blood when provoked. At least that was what the more fearful ones called him, the two or three he had managed to intimidate over the past few years. But where were even those few when "The Shark" was a captive for three days in the county jail? He smiled a sad smile. No doubt they thought he could crash his way out, ripping through the steel bars as if they were the chalk-brittle bones of humans. To all others he was mostly Mote. He was a man who could tell a good joke every now and then and never carried a weapon.

At first the bus seemed the reasonable way to get home. He had eleven dollars in his pocket, more than enough for a one-way ticket. With no one meeting him upon his release he briefly thought of hitchhiking back as some form of revenge. Certainly a cab was out of the question. That was the way Badfoot Tony came home after a night in the Dayton jail, stepping from a Yellow Cab with grand lies, ready to keep everyone laughing all summer long. But less than twenty minutes ago the bus ticket agent had told Mote that he had just missed the last bus north for three hours.

"Cutbacks," the man said, scratching grizzle, then shrugging. "Hey, what can you do?"

Mote could be nearly home in three hours. By car he was only twenty minutes from Big Edna's front door, the only home he knew. In the dull light of late morning he had talked softly to himself.

"Yeah, I can hitch me a ride home in all that time and save my scratch for a juicy Big Boy." He easily conjured the smell of french fries and the special sauce of the double-decker hamburger oozing warmly down his thumb.

The downtown streets of Butler had been quiet with only a few shoppers strolling in the late Thursday morning, occasional cars for traffic. Just three blocks from the county jail he had started sweating. Against his back rode the bright green suit which he carried on a hanger, one finger hooking its curved end. He had paused, spotted a dry cleaner's shop, and moved toward it. He pushed inside with a smile on his face. A middle-aged woman stood behind the counter, writing quickly across pink receipts.

"Excuse me, Miss, but do y'all got a extra bag I could buy?"

The woman looked up, leaned, then smiled. "Just for that one suit? Why, I think we can scare up a little old bag." She took the suit and hanger from him and placed it on a tall metal hook next to the cash register. He smelled a faint lemon perfume, noticed her tight jeans. Like drawing a curtain, she tore off a swath of cellophane, pinched an opening, and quickly covered the suit.

"This do?" she asked. The diamonds in her wedding ring stunned him.

He was holding the suit again before he spoke. "Yes, yes, this'll do just fine. Keep the dust and bugs off the suit, you know."

"What kind of cleaner's you go to don't give you a bag?" she asked.

"Well, they was running just a little short this morning, I do believe."

She waved a finger. "You just think of us first next time. No way we send a customer out with his suit clean but naked to the breeze."

The suit was not clean. If she had looked harder, she might have seen the smudges at the front pockets of the trousers, the spot on the front coat sleeve made from a dollop of coleslaw, maybe. Might have smelled, too, if she leaned very close, the dried perspiration, not his, like the smell of iron at the armpits of the suit. If she did notice any of this, she was too kind to say so and very shrewd at drumming up business.

At the first intersection he found an empty public phone booth, ran a finger around the coin return, then stepped back with a frown. After the bad news at the station he had begun to walk with purpose. For the next few blocks, he put up his thumb, not even turning when he heard traffic approaching from the rear. There were no takers. Though his luck was always mixed weather, he had a feeling that rain was his only future ahead.

Soon the businesses—the quick-change tire places, the one-story motels and bars—had thinned out, and the four-lane avenue through the city quieted to the highway to Union City and points north. He passed the last of the burger and fries places already floating its rich smell to the morning, a smell that weakened his knees. That morning for breakfast he had oatmeal, warm milk, and limp toast with just the threat of butter. He swallowed and again resolved not to stop yet for food. But he remembered joking with one of the trustees, a wiry man the world had nicknamed "Forty."

"Least a man about to be set free ought to have a meal to remember y'all by," Mote had said.

Forty had nodded and attempted a smile. "Such a man ought to get a meal that'll teach his dumb ass to stay out of jail." Forty reached around for a palm to slap. None offered. Around them other prisoners ate, traded jokes or baseball stories. One or two stared into space.

"I bet that's what keep you here, Forty," he said. "You crazy about the oatmeal."

"Go to hell, Cox," the wiry man had said. "I done you one favor cutting you in on the tonk game. I don't owe you a damned thing else."

Mote had finished his breakfast, then chuckled as he backed out of the noisy room. He would be a free man within an hour, never to see Forty again, at least in drab jailhouse issue.

Mote's grand wish for the day was to get home before his aunt Edna returned from her job. Thursdays were the days she sat on the front porch immediately after work, talking loudly with Miss Hester or any of the other women walking past the house. If he got home too late, his shame would be very public, halting conversation or laughter. No, he would much prefer to be home first, to suffer wrath behind closed doors for a day or so.

One car honked as it sped past, someone whooped from another. Then a car slowed, a 1975 Pontiac with a dented rear fender, one end tied to the car body with two wire coat hangers. A front tire bumped the curb twice, shaking the fender. A man in a cowboy hat leaned out.

"Can I get you anywhere, partner?"

"I'm going ten miles up the road," Mote said.

"Well, I can't take you that far, but I can get you three, four miles closer anyway."

The inside of the Bonneville smelled of equal parts cigarette smoke and pine. The driver slapped the top of the dashboard as they rolled away.

"Can't provide you much entertainment on account the radio's busted. Been after my brother-in-law to fix the dad-blamed thing, but you can't squeeze water from a rock. When he ain't half-working or racing cars around the mud track over there in Franklin, he home on the back porch drinking beer."

Mote smiled. He noticed a long scar across the back of the stranger's hand. Then the man nodded to his suit hanging behind Mote. The plastic rippled in the wind coming through the back window.

"Nice suit you got there," the man said. "You headed somewheres special, I bet. A wedding?"

"No." The last of the neighborhoods were thinning out to the cornfields north of Butler. He was still sweating from the walking.

"No, there's a big dance coming up tonight and they can't start without me."

The man slapped the wheel this time and laughed loudly. "You mean to tell me I'm driving around a full-blown celebrity?"

Mote figured the man on his own could quickly conclude that celebrities do not take ten-mile hikes on weekday mornings, that they hitchhike only if their shiny new cars break down in a cloud of smoke.

"Well, I don't know about all that," Mote said. He then proceeded to tell the man about his release from a hospital. Minor surgery on his back, three days' recovery, and now a clean bill of health.

"Man, that can't be no fun someone cutting on your back and now you having to walk and all. By the way, the name's Youstler. Good friends just call me Vernon."

Mote took the offered hand and introduced himself. Then he asked, "You live back there in Butler?"

"Me? Uh-uh. I was just checking on a horse a old boy wants to sell me. Horse he showed me wasn't in too good a shape, if you want to know the truth. Me, I live on a farm just up a ways here. Got a few cows and horses, but mostly corn, you know. But a fellow can't hardly make it farming these days. That's how come my car damned near older than my marriage."

Vernon Youstler spat out of his window. "You surely welcome to drop in and have lunch with me and my wife. Nothing's ever fancy on our table, but it sticks to your ribs, if you know what I mean."

"I'm in a big hurry to get home." He glanced at Youstler. "I thank you much for your invitation."

"Suit yourself. Remember the welcome mat's out and you got a couple more miles to think about it."

Mote was tempted to take up the offer. Among bright fields he might find a boisterous place—dogs barking, radio loud from inside the house, the riot of children at play. Inside, the house might smell of fried onions, his favorite smell next to french fries. He could eat there, nap surely, then be back on the highway in less than ninety minutes. But no, no. Big Edna might be home early. Besides, instead of a lunch so efficiently prepared, he might be there alone, this Youstler. He might have chased a son into the Air Force, a daughter to a husband who apologized for work, and a wife who fled to her parents. Yes, this very driver could be in a house alone, moaning into the night, or murdering strangers who hitchhiked into the small circle he stalked and counting their severed toes each midnight. Crazy folks were everywhere these days, Mote had long concluded. He did not need newspapers to tell him that.

At the turnoff, Mote thanked the man, lifted out his suit. Youstler presented him with a ripe orange. "Don't do anything I wouldn't do." Then he waved and roared off down a gravel road that seemed to have no end, but curved sharply into a grove of maples.

Mote pushed the orange into a back pocket, then moved on. By the time he had regained his original walking speed, the memory of jail washed back over him. During the first night there he wondered about his stupid acts from the past—stealing hubcaps, car batteries. In the near dark he regretted for the first time stealing fruit from the large outdoor bins that ringed the closest Krogers, regretted the fruit trees robbed, then running with friends down alleys, prompted by the curses of the tree owners or the sound of a shotgun shell pumped into a chamber. Such petty things. In jail he heard of even grander schemes, of plots that would retire men before they were forty years of age. All around him those few days were men, twenty to twenty-five years old, all moving in and out, who were there only because of bad luck or a mental lapse.

("I forgot to put the damn mask on before I got up to the counter. She must have hit the button while I was pulling it on.")

("How was I to know somebody was at home? I counted two cars at the place, so they're both gone, see? And the same top light is on like when they're away. I'm halfway in the back door when the light goes on. I haul ass but they still got a good look at me some kind of way, know what I'm saying? Wasn't for the bad luck, the stuff would be fenced and I'd be in Cleveland somewhere ordering drinks for the whole goddamned bar.")

("My luck, the homeless guy wanting a spoon is narco.")

("My idea was to shoot out the bank camera. So I come in behind a couple people, then I slide along the wall. When I'm just under the camera, I pop up and give a hit. But the first shot misses, see? The second one gets it good. My partner got everybody covered. Well, we get the money and run. But next morning my picture on the front page, showing sparks from the gun and shit.

I'm at my girlfriend's on my second can of root beer when they bust in.")

Quirks of fate herded them together, nothing more. The county jail smelled of Lifebuoy soap and piss. The stances of the ones in for the first time amused him, like high schoolers posing in front of lockers before the first bell. Mote imitated the veterans, relaxed before the start of the shift at the steel mill. A few called each other by first name. Mote spoke to them all upon eye contact. "Hey, slick," he'd say or "What's up?" Someone told him to never smile in the holding tank. Ask and give no favors. No one in there could be your friend.

But where had his friends been? He knew now that a few of them, those without full-time jobs, would be hanging around the park playing bid whist or a lazy game of basketball. Swine, a sec- ond-shift man, would be washing his new car. Mote would tell them all a thing or two about friendship and loyalty. After all, friends are the ones who show up.

He stopped at a service station at a crossroads. Although it was a numbered county road, Edna had called it, as from some ancient time, "Princeton Pike." At the cash register he asked for the key to the men's room.

The clerk, a skinny man with a smudge on his chin, was talking to himself as he attended to a credit-card purchase. Then: "The men's bathroom been closed down since Monday. You buying gas?"

"No," Mote said.

The clerk looked up, shook his head, then pointed. "Take the women's key there."

Afterwards he bought a soda. The clerk scooped up the coins. "How far you going, guy?"

"Just up the highway a little bit and I'm done."

"Lucky you," the man said. "I have to sit here all day and deal with farmers and fools. Nice suit there."

"Thank you." The man yawned, closed his eyes and stretched. Mote smoothly palmed a cigarette lighter from the display next to the Swisher Sweets and left.

The next stretch of highway looked hotter. The sun had broken through the cloud cover, and for a half mile or so there were cornfields flowing away from both sides of the road. Two crows banked high overhead. The median separating the lanes was a long narrow island of knee-high weeds. He seemed to startle battalions of flies every half mile or so, as they would dive at the sides of his head or the back of his neck.

Three miles from the service station he stopped, lay the suit down carefully on the ground, and tied his shoes. Then he glanced at his watch. It had stopped again. Moving again, he calculated that it must have stopped about the time he had parted with Youstler. Next time he gambled, he would gamble for a watch.

Big Edna had not even bothered to see him in jail. Years before when he first got into trouble, the police called her to the station. She warned him then: "I'll come get you once, but I ain't doing it two times. If you want to make the jail your hotel, you go right ahead. But don't count on me as one of your visitors."

And he didn't. After the first rough scrapes at the Palm Grill, those tussling matches in the alley between Irwin's barbershop and Moore's Fix-It-Rite Garage, the police got to know him and would glance his way when they passed in their squad cars. He knew their faces, too, and recognized one when he was picked up three days ago for fighting loud Frazier about something as silly as clothes. They had broken up the party with their tussling and had been separated by the time the police showed. Darlene had gone on and on about the broken furniture and her parents away in Detroit. She told the two officers that both men were crashers, that they had slipped in uninvited while she was not looking. That part was easy. After all, Frazier was known to keep a gun in his car for bluff and stayed in trouble. But this time Frazier got six stitches to the head from hitting the corner of the table. Mote got two nights in jail.

Passing on the other side of the highway was a small tribe of children—loud with their music. During breaks in the traffic, one or two of them would step to the pavement, dance a step or two. When they drew even with him, one picked up a rock and faked a throw at him. Mote did not budge. He had counted eight of them. Young mad dogs, he thought. Out here, if the lead dog bolts for him the rest would follow, risking traffic. But their music drew them on. The boy threw the rock, which sailed far overhead.

He had stopped in front of a farm of scotch pines, the tallest no higher than four feet. They were planted in straight, even rows.

The symmetry of their diagonals was dazzling. He climbed over a wire fence and picked out a tree in the fourth row from the road. He laid down the suit, smoothed the plastic. He found the orange Youstler had given him, peeled it with his thumbnail, and slowly ate it, standing.

Two moving vans sped by in succession, heading south. Within minutes, the vans would pick up the state road that would take them to US 75 and from there—who knows? On a map he once traced the highway from northern Michigan to Orlando, Florida. Along the way were Detroit, Toledo, Dayton (the furthest north he had been), Cincinnati, Lexington, Kentucky (the furthest south he had been, to an uncle's rambling house in the country), Knoxville, Atlanta, Macon, Valdosta—all faraway places he could only imagine, places he could not even conjure smells for. At night there had been the many times that he wanted—upon hearing the 11:10 freight train following its tracks along the river and him loving the mournful horn sounding—he wanted to risk his life and hop one of the moving cars. He would ride it to wherever it stopped in the morning, the break of day as the only destination.

He started now to hum "Jimmy Mack," one of Big Edna's favorite songs. Actually, her favorite. She could be at the sink, slicing onions or dragging strips of beef liver through flour or turning okra coated with cornmeal in the frying pan, all the while she sang this song. Singing loudly to herself, she would roll her shoulders. Or she would find the old 45 record and listen to it through its storm of scratches. She never explained if and how the song made any real difference in her life. Who was her Jimmy Mack?

My arms are missing you, my lips feel the same way, too-oo.

In the song a woman misses her lover. At the same time she is wooed mightily by another man. Mote knew nothing of Edna's earlier personal life. He had found two photographs once of two different men. One was in a military uniform. The other leaned against the back of a convertible, arms crossed, legs crossed at the ankles. Both were smiling while frowning into the sun.

Less of a mystery was her caution and strict discipline. He remembered those nights in high school when he managed to slip away from house arrest to house parties or out-of-town roller rinks. He would return half-expecting her to be singing the song from some corner of the house. More frequently than not, she would be asleep in a chair in front of the television, shadows flitting across her face and around the walls like butterflies of the night.

A wedding party of three cars went past—old dented cars honking, the lead car with "Just Married" soaped on its windows. The drivers looked young, barely older than the tribe walking south. What was the urgency that they could not wait until Saturday? How much time could the groom get off from his mill shift? Where was the honeymoon?

Mote chewed a couple slivers of orange rind. He took out the stolen lighter, flipped on the flame, closed the cap. Did it again. Then he stood to move on, getting less than two hundred yards, where he found a road leading away. An iron bridge crossed a creek just fifty yards down. He figured one other stop would be enough and he would still get home ahead of Big Edna. Within minutes he was sitting on the edge of the bridge, his feet dangling, then kicking like a child's from the lip of a playground swing, his suit carefully folded and lying in the road behind him. The creek rolled away beneath him, every now and then a stray paper cup pushed along by the current. He saw no fish, but there were large minnows silvering across and against the current. He could still hear the stray cars and trucks along State Route 4.

From the other end of the bridge, with the magical quiet of deer, a man and a boy emerged—a grandfather and grandson, Mote figured—with bamboo poles and each with a coffee can.

Mote waved. "How y'all?" Where had they come from?

They waved back. He watched them pull night crawlers from their cans and bait their hooks for what seemed like an eternity. When they finally dropped their lines into the water, he lay back and closed his eyes. The sunlight slanting through the trees colored the insides of his eyelids. Yes, he would rest here a short spell.

Then: "I bet you're patching up a marriage," Mote heard. He stiffened though his eyes stayed closed. Maybe the man was playing some kind of game.

"Good try, but you missed by a mile if you talking to me."

"Can't blame a soul for trying." The man laughed.

"What y'all fishing for?" Mote asked.

"We fishing for whatever bite," the man said. "We ain't particular. 'Course a couple big catfish and ten, twelve bluegill wouldn't be too bad."

Mote stretched his arms out backward behind him. His body took up one lane. The man spoke again. "Mister, I don't know who you is, but you might want to sit up over there. A car come along and take your head and arms off, both."

"You wouldn't tell me if a car was coming?"

"I might be too busy with a big fish to notice," the man said.

Mote chuckled and opened his eyes. Out on the highway he could hear an eighteen-wheeler heading north, followed by something with a broken muffler. Then it was quiet before he heard a splash in the water. The man had just cast and was shaking his line with his free hand. The man spoke without turning.

"You laying there like that remind me of another man and another bridge about thirty years ago. Man come up on me while I was fishing down home. I was using dough balls that day, and he ain't never seen that before. They the best things in the world for catching catfish, let me tell you. Anyway he say new to Alabama, that he was from up north, Illinois, Indiana, one. He did say that he was down there to register voters and start some kind of school to teach folks to read so they can take the voting tests and remember the Constitution if they was asked. He claimed there was two or three of them moving around the county doing such."

The man paused, said something to the boy. Then he cleared his throat and spat into the water below.

"That was his answer to my first question about what he was doing in Alabama. My second was did he have any kinfolks closeby. He said no. Then he haul off and say we all brothers and sisters anyway. That 'bout beat all. I mean, I expects all us colored is brothers and sisters in a way, but saying it don't make folks believe it or act like they believe it.

"Then I asked him if he was carrying any protection. He said no again. Said he was unarmed. Then I told him a little about the history where he was at, but he just shake his head like he heard it all before. I told him trees got eyes and rivers got rooms. Then he just got on up and dusted his butt. He thanked me real nice for my time and went on his way. Things commenced to get real hot around home when a few in our part of the county tried to vote. I did hear tell about one or two thrown in jail. Next year a few more did vote, then more after that. I never did vote until I come up north. I come up to help my sister's family when she got down with the arthritis so bad. I got a job at the mill and voted for the first time. Every time I vote or fish I think of that young man down there walking around with no protection. Do something like that strangers and you done something for true. Never did get his name. What's your name?"

"All my friends call me Mote."

"I'm Jesse, and this here Lake." There was a splash, and they both turned to look.

"I got one." It was a man's voice, not a boy's. Jesse coaxed Lake to pull it up with force, not to let it run too far for cover. The dwarf yanked his fish out of the water and swung it up to the bridge. Jesse patted the small man on the head, then unhooked the fish.

"Ain't that a beauty?" He held the fish high, its tail curling. "Oh, wait, Mister. You want a fish? We gon' have plenty by the time we leave today." Mote was tempted. He could clean it and have it soaking in lemon juice by the time Edna got home. She could fry it tomorrow, hushpuppies on the side.

"Yes," he finally said. Jesse wrapped it in newspaper and presented it to him as if offering a trophy. Mote thanked him, picked up his suit, and said his farewell.

"You got more to do than listen a old man go on and on, sho. You probably got a wife and children home waiting. Say, that's a fine suit you got there. I was joking a while ago about you and a bad marriage. Now I see the suit, you might be going to a wedding."

"You getting warm, Jesse. I'm actually headed to a reunion, my high school reunion."

"I thought it was something like that, sho. Well, you be particular."

Jesse was smiling, Lake's face was a stone.

He reentered the world of waking, rushing, highway afternoon traffic. The three o'clock light was flat, but glare ahead gone. A car passed in a smear of a horn blast, its wake lifting the hem of the suit coat. He tried to hold the fish, still moving, like a football, his hand gripping it under the head. He tried to imagine a tie and shirt to match the suit. Maybe he would find a silk square to let spill out of the breast pocket. A bright gold would catch the ladies' attention. He remembered lawyers standing in line at First National Bank with matching ties and silk squares. Such combinations announced that they knew their way around banks and airports and golf courses. These men did not fold their squares neatly to that sawtooth edge that Deacon Davis might use. Theirs looked careless, pushed into the pocket with three fingers. Mote preferred theirs. He would surprise his friends at the North Star Cafe one night. Oh yes, they would pinch it, poke it, and have their fun. But would take a step back in their minds and straighten up with admiration.

He smiled. He was much closer to home now, and he had won a card game and a suit, even if it had been in jail. It had just been a few hours ago that he and a man known in Butler and Union City as Late Hit were released. They arrived at the supply room at the same time. Late Hit, taller and stouter with a red bandanna tied around his head, checked through his pouch of belongings with the patience of a monk. The suit was rolled up in another pouch. He looked at Mote, then scratched his chin as he handed it over.

"Sure you don't want to play another hand?" he asked. "I'll throw in a bus ticket home if you beat me this time."

"I got my people out front any minute now."

Late Hit had chuckled. "This suit is magic, but I got ten, twelve like it. I was just trying to save you a little trouble. Women like to touch it, rub up against it. A country boy like you might not know what to do in it."

"I'll just have to take that chance. Let me know when you ready to lose another." Mote had changed into his wrinkled clothes in a restroom. As he came down the steps, folding the job list, he passed the intake area. He noticed a woman heavily perfumed. She wore tight peach slacks and a sleeveless white blouse. She carried a brown paper bag, paused to look at the suit he was carrying, and hurried up the stairs, muttering something.

Above Mote now floated a billboard warning drivers to buckle their seatbelts. Another pleaded for attention to the latest home mortgage rates. Nearer to town, the road kills thickened—raccoon, two possums, a small dog on its back, three stiff legs to the sky, no sign of the other. A siren or two sounded from somewhere ahead. A Greyhound bus roared past, heading in his same direction. Then he descended to the town where he had grown up.

He crossed an overpass. Up ahead, about a mile or so at Douglas Park, he would find Nora and Teddy, the all-day wino lovers. There would be the swimming pool with its chatter, laughter, and splashing drifting on the wind. Big Edna would have mousetraps still set, one just inside the back door, the other at the base of a food cabinet near the chipped corner of the door that never quite closed. The house might smell of...He slowed just two blocks from home, imagining. Cabbage, mustard greens? No, no. Cabbage was a Monday kind of smell. Friday was most often fried fish. But Thursday?

Past the park and its roaring mythologies, past the dying corner market where cheap wine sold best in the late afternoons, donuts until midmorning, and bologna and saltines in between—past all this he gained the alley just past the newly renovated church. In one backyard a lazy terrier, Rope-a-Dope, lay on the roof of his house. But farther down a caged Doberman lunged at him. He stepped closer, wondering if the dog had caught the scent of the fish, but then moved on.

"Welcome home," he said softly to the backs of the narrow houses he was now passing—pink, green, off-white—with their fences in varying degrees of disrepair. "Ain't exactly Mr. Rogers."

At the back door, he paused, then let himself in, avoiding the mousetraps. He had a snack of milk and cookies. Then he cleaned the fish, pulling away its skin with pliers. He cut a lemon in half and squeezed both halves over the fish. He set the platter with the fish in the refrigerator and covered it with waxed paper. In his room he hung the suit on the inside doorknob, then collapsed to his hard bed. Before dropping off to sleep, he remembered that the house smelled of fried bacon.

When he awoke it was almost dark, and he could see light beneath the bedroom door. The radio in the kitchen was on loud. It was a news program, and the announcer's description of a Cincinnati expressway pile-up sounded like news about a war. Mote could hear, too, his aunt opening and closing cabinet doors.

When he walked into the kitchen, she continued to move around. From the clock he figured he had slept three hours. He was still sore from the walk—his feet and hamstrings, mostly. He found a clean jelly jar and turned on the cold water at the sink.

"Hi," he said.

She was a large, dark brown woman with evenly graying, short hair. She kept moving, measuring out a cup of flour, then pouring it into a large mixing bowl. She broke two eggs against the counter and dropped the yolks and whites into the bowl. Tossed the shells underhanded to the trash bin. She turned down the radio.

"Hi," he tried again.

This time she stopped, her back still to him. "Where is your God?" She was standing at the short leg of an L-shaped counter, and he could look over her shoulder to a vacant lot across the alley. Surely, something there had prompted the question.

"I asked you a question, Michael Otis Cox."

"My...God? I don't know what you mean."

"Oh yes you do. You must know where your God is if you walk right in from the jailhouse into my kitchen and drink a glass of water like it's the most natural thing in the world. You got to know where your protection is. You got to know something."

"Miss Edna, I'm sorry..."

"Sorry ain't enough. Sorry didn't put you in jail. Sorry didn't make the bed you got to lay down in." She paused. "I know about the fight, yeah, all about it. News travel in this town quicker than stink off cow shit."

She stopped talking and turned back to making what he hoped and prayed were biscuits. The radio announcer was now on the baseball scores. He swallowed the last of the water and set his glass down. In another normal time he would make a ham sandwich even with dinner just an hour away. But now was not normal.

"You still didn't tell me nothing about your God."

"What's God got to do with it?"

"Your God don't know your mind?"

He shrugged. "Maybe I don't know my own mind. Can God know my mind, if I don't?" He felt dizzy and sat on a rickety stepstool.

"Well, you better get to know your mind quick, Mr. Man. I told you the first time the police pick you up that I ain't having that in this house."

"I'll be back at the mill..."

"This ain't New Year's Eve," she said, "and I ain't in the mood for no empty promises."

"They ain't empty."

"Well, you gone have to show me something." She was rolling out the dough flat, sprinkling out more flour, pausing to pull splotches of moist dough off the rolling pin.

"I need me some collateral. You know how you can go to the bank and ask for a loan and the man ask what you can put up against that amount in case you can't keep up the payments?"

He had never applied for a loan in his life. The only car he had owned he had bought for two hundred dollars cash. He leaned back on the stool as she talked about shame and responsibility and gratitude, as she cut out her biscuits and arranged them meticulously on the baking sheet. He wanted to close his eyes ever so slightly, but dared not. He wanted to stand, raise his right hand, and shout to the world, "I stand guilty as accused," but knew it could not be that easy. He listened, heard his histories. What was there to argue with? He had been in jail three days, with near-empty pockets walked most of the way home, and now sat in the kitchen of the only person who ever loved him. He needed her love and touch as much as her biscuits.

"So you tell me what you want to do for credit, then we can move on."

"I don't understand," he said.

"Well, you could stand in the middle of Eighteenth Avenue and tell the world you're sorry to act so stupid, to embarrass your sainted mama, Bernice, and your daddy, Anthony, and grandfolks, all of them gone from this life. You could tell the world that, you."

Mote frowned. Slow walkers to and from Jackson's corner grocery store—a lollipop or Coke or cheap wine in a brown bag for their troubles—all might stand and watch his confession, loud and public, as they might watch a gospel melody sung by a collie. And what of his friends when word got out about such a confession? Could such shame be forgiven and forgotten?

"...and don't come thinking about going to church with your head hanging. Unless you want to stand up in front of the church and tell all."

He could see himself there with the small humble group who

came forward for special prayers. On his rare mornings in church he had wondered at their sins, what brought them forward? He had watched their backs, studied the runover heels of their shoes. If he stood up there alone, Jimmie, the organ player, might pause and watch all with a faint smile. The choir would sit back, eyes shrouded, a jury in their magnificent powder-blue satin robes. The minister and his assistant would sit perfectly still as he went to the start of the fight. He would tell them about protecting his honor, about the exaggerated fear of the hostess. Of jail there was little to speak; of the suit, nothing. Members of the deacon board in their somber grays and browns would nod, and one, Deacon Williams, would urge him to tell all.

"Tell it to the Lord and loving witnesses, son," he would whisper fiercely. Then repeat the command in a booming voice that would wash awake the audience, the street outside, the park where someone might be sleeping on a picnic table at that very moment.

Mote would keep his eyes to the rear of the church, just above the heads of the usherettes standing across the back, especially above Janine, a young high schooler bursting now into her womanhood.

Mote got up to refill his glass. "I don't know. I ain't never spoke in front of people before."

"Talk to them like they family," she said.

But they were not family, he knew. She was the only family he had known, and he could not speak long to her. Those outside were strangers who cut their grass or sat on their front porches talking and laughing and watching the world ease past. He would much rather confess before strangers he would never see again— at the shopping mall fountain or a bus terminal.

"You see, I got to live here, even if you don't. I want them to know that Edna did her best, always did the best she could."

"Ain't there some other way, something else I could do?" he asked. "What do they care?"

She put the sheet into the oven and wiped her hands on a towel. "You figure out what to do. It just have to be something more than you saying you won't do it again just in this house."

"Damn," he whispered.

"What you say?" She looked at him directly.

139

"I didn't say nothing." He went to his room. There he lay on his back, one arm over his eyes. At least she did not ask about the fish. His radio played thin anthems of loss. Blues of the Jimmy Reed–Howling Wolf variety saddened him whenever Big Edna played them on her ancient stereo. But the up-to-date sad songs only bothered him like the difference between the last two women he had been with. Heavy-hipped Carol aroused him with just one look. He could remember whole conversations with her and on some days missed her so much he ached all over. Jackie was much prettier, drew stares when she showed up in bright, short dresses. Yet away from her he had to strain to recall her face, her voice. The old music was not pretty to him, but, despite himself, he could sing aloud lines from a few of them. The new blues left him blank. Strange, he thought now, how all that worked.

He remembered a line from a woman's song:

> I've been trying hard to be true,
> But Jimmy, he talks just as sweet as you
> Jimmy, oh Jimmy, hey, Jimmy Mack,
> When are you coming back?

Then he thought about calling one of his friends, but did not. From outside, front, he heard voices, then a car with a thunderous bass. He rolled to his side, still sore, and drifted off.

"Dinner ready."

He opened his eyes to find a thin shaft of light in the room. He did not turn over. "I ain't hungry now. I'll eat a little something later."

There was a pause, music rushing into the room, warmer than wind. She knew his affection for angel biscuits. She knew he did not have that much discipline where food was concerned. He heard the rustle of the plastic bag over his suit. He still did not turn over.

"It's your stomach," she said and closed the door.

He had persuaded himself that this would hurt her more than anything else. Within the hour, surely, she would beg him to eat. She might not forgive him, true. If he decided to leave, he would not be turned around this time, that much was clear. And if he stayed, to the neighbors he would blame jail on his age, on the fact that his parents, both of them, had vanished like smoke from this land. He drifted in and out of sleep for a couple hours. He thought of Jesse and Lake and the fish they probably caught. He remembered the old man carrying memories as easily as a can of live bait.

He was surprised when she did not beg him to eat. He was more surprised at her voice when she shouted good night from deep within the house. He could hear her close her bedroom door, heard the light switch click, and after counting to five hundred, was up. Edna slept heavily. Whole storms could boil up in the night and pound the land, and she would awaken in the morning, marveling only at the peace in some bright morning.

But he was up. He threw everything he could into a small suitcase from under the bed. He would return for whatever was left behind. Maybe get back one day when she was away at work. He moved through the dark kitchen, catching his hip on the corner of the countertop. He closed the back door quietly. No mousetrap sounded.

Outside it was warm and still. One or two dogs started up. One or two cars sped past the end of the alley. He walked with no idea of where he was going and who would take him in. He would go to the park and think about it.

At the mouth of the alley, a car stopped. He could hear a blast of music before it wilted. It was True and Pepper, True at the wheel. He could smell the rum. He did not lower his bag or look at them at first.

"Mote, is that you, man? Where you going with that bag this time of night?" Pepper wore dark glasses even at night. He went on. "So jail can be rough, can't it? Look, don't worry about Frazier. We'll back you if he start anything."

True leaned from the steering wheel. "Hey, hey, yeah, Mote, tell us that joke, you know the one about the badfoot nigger from Alabama..."

"Fuck y'all," Mote said. "Fuck all, y'all."

They roared off with laughs to awake the night. He walked home through a chorus of barking dogs.

Back in his room he slept for only an hour, it seemed. Mote stood up and paced around his room, his bag still packed. Then he ate his cereal in the silent kitchen. He was rinsing his bowl in the sink when he heard the creaking.

"Morning," he said, not turning.

"Morning." She turned on the radio and found a station that played country music.

He smiled. There was no figuring his aunt. "No 'Jimmy Mack'?" he asked.

"Maybe by noon."

"I been all the time meaning to ask you how come you like that song so much." He was fishing out a cold biscuit and looking for a jar of honey.

"It reminds me of my dancing days, is all." She paused. "I just loved to go dancing, especially at the park dances outdoors at night. All that was gone by the time you grew up."

"You never know somebody in real life like the guy in the song?"

She laughed. "I knew a few men like him, but I wouldn't call them back."

He nodded. "If you turn down that hee-haw stuff, I'll tell you something."

She took her time. She poured more sugar into her coffee, tasted it, poured a bit more.

"You know that ain't good for you," Mote said.

"You my doctor?" She took a long sip, then turned down a radio ballad about too much whiskey and too little love.

He cleared his throat. "You ever hear the saying 'The trees got ears and the river got rooms'?"

She shrugged. "Never have. Sounds like to me somebody saying be careful. Where you hear something country like that?"

"Some old man."

"Was that all you wanted to tell me?"

"Well, what if I went to just some of neighbors, you know, and kind of explained about the circumstances? Would that satisfy you? I mean, they could pass it on to the others."

She took another sip, frowning against the cup's warmth. "Cover both sides of the street on this block from end to end—'course you can skip the Tatums. They might shoot at you the way they shot at the Wilhite boy last Halloween. Do that and I'll be happy."

He sighed and closed his eyes. "Okay, okay."

She was in front of him. She clicked her cup against the empty bowl he was drying off, toasted him the way she did when he announced his first after-school job, when he announced his breakup from Mary Alice, whose mother she never liked, when he announced seven years ago that he might join the church.

She was smiling. "They got me working this morning. It's Friday so it's some extra pay. I be back home from work around five-thirty. I want you to start with the neighbors while I'm gone. You know all their schedules. Then tonight me and you start back on the story about your suit..."

"Oh, there really ain't nothing to tell."

She reached for her sweater and purse. "I don't have time now. I got to get to work."

"Okay," he said.

"You go ahead and start the fish, too. Use that beer batter I showed you that time and go heavy on the garlic salt. I'll fix up a little something on the side when I get back. You sure picked yourself out a nice-sized fish."

She was nearly out of the door when she turned. "Maybe this evening when you all through, I'll tell you something about my Jimmy Mack." The screen door slammed, and he watched her go down the front steps. She stopped, turned to make sure her slip was not hanging, then moved on. He shook his head, was all he could do.

El Balserito

Because my Spanish is chips-and-salsa simple, and I am desirous
of improving upon it, and delighted whenever I can puzzle out on
my own some new word or phrase, I am listening in on the con-
versation of the two Cuban men next to me at the counter of the
plumbing supply store in Little Haiti, and when I hear the word
balserito I recognize this to be a diminutive of *balsero,* "the rafter,"
that symbol of the Cuban-American experience, those cast ashore
on scrap-wood rafts emblematic of an entire community's exile,
and when the one man goes out to his truck and comes back with
a little plastic dashboard toy of Goofy and another Disney charac-
ter floating in an inner tube, and the other man, laughing and
smiling at the joke asks, *Quien es, el otro?,* pointing at the smaller
figure, I know that this is Max, Goofy's son, because we have just
taken Sam to see *A Goofy Movie,* a story of father-son bonding in
the cartoon universe, a universe in many ways more familiar to
me than this one, though of course I say nothing to the men, not
wanting to admit I have been eavesdropping, or betray my lin-
guistic insufficiency, the degree to which I am an outsider here, in
Miami, a place unlike any other I have known, a city we have
fixed upon like Rust Belt refugees eager to buy a little piece of the
sunshine, to mortgage a corner of the American Dream, where
already Sam has begun to master the local customs, youngest and
most flexible, first to make landfall, betraying the generational
nature of acculturation the way the poems of my students at the
state university do, caught between past and present worlds,
transplanted parents looking back to Havana while the children
are native grown, rooted to the soil, though the roots of *las pal-
mas* are notoriously shallow, hence their propensity to topple in a
hurricane, tropical storm, even the steady winter trade wind bear-
ing its flotilla of makeshift sails across the Straits of Florida, so
many this season that some mornings, jogging along the board-
walk in the shadows of the luxury hotels, I have come upon three
rafts washed up in a single mile of beach, ragged planks and Sty-

rofoam and chicken wire, filthy and abandoned but curiously empowered, endowed with a violent, residual energy, like shotgun casings in a field of corn stubble or the ruptured jelly of turtle eggs among mangroves, chrysalides discarded as the cost of the journey, shells of arrival, shells of departure.

Alba: Innocence

Sunday. The bells, as expected. I cannot
help it if I rise, if finding the room too
fraught with light—all of it, the white
walls, the rinsed notion (always almost

inside then just out of reach) of God, your
body gleaming in sleep where the sun falls
on it and away from, falls on and away—
I have to shut my one good eye and at once

the leaves falling but now blurred make it
possible to see how it happens, a bruise
lifting itself over time from the darker
blues to, slowly, something like amber,

to at last whatever, before the wounding,
the flesh was. Imagining the flesh before
or without knowledge, I want to say it is
most like song untrained, whose beauty,

when it occurs, surprises even itself—
but isn't it also, more commonly, just
meat, or isn't it good soil waiting, that
does not, cannot know that it is waiting?

Therefore, it is innocence. Therefore,
a capacity for suffering more vast, even,
than the landscape whose particulars, you
remember, we drove past, the red of sunset

upon them: the bull in mid-lumbering over
the cow (still with patience, with fear?),
almost, not yet inside her; the sudden
bursting of crows, all cinders flying over

where once, presumably, was some small life.
We were tired, hungry, faintly hungry for
each other. We kept driving: east, home,
toward a dark we couldn't fast enough get to.

Ti Kikit

Ti Kikit puts on some pink lipstick,
stands on the Place Saint-Pierre in Pétionville.
For this evening she has borrowed a friend's
plastic barrettes, eleven of them, each pinching
a spongy braid at its base, dotting her head
with pink. She likes that corner
of the Choucoune Hotel—white bougainvilleas overflow
from behind the walls, make her feel pretty
while she waits. Her real name is Rose;
her aunt Aséfi named her Ti Kikit
after the small brown bird. Aunt Aséfi
was not really family but raised
her for eight years after the orphan appeared
on the road in front of her house.
Ti Kikit earned the small bird's name
when the thick rope she used to try hanging
herself left a gray scar around her neck.
It looks just like the bird's markings.
                    Hey bitch? Yeah, you! How much you charge for it?!
Forty cents...
Wait here! Yeah, there! We are coming for you!
Okay forty cents! But the four of us!
Ti Kikit tries to argue. They grab her
shoulders, push her down over the car trunk,
pull her short skirt up, bare her tiny ass.
The biggest boy shoves himself inside her.
The blood makes him see he is her first.
                    Hey bitch? Remember my name is François!
Ti Kikit's face is crushed on the windshield,
eyes dilated, white. She remembers Aséfi's well
and Bourik, the mule, which tail-whipped
all day long black flies from its genitals
and from that raw spot on her back

the wooden saddle kept enlarging. One day
her aunt held her face, told her, "Be good":
she could not take care of her anymore but
be good. Ti Kikit's mind goes to the one sheep her mother
ever owned, the day she gave it to the Spirits
as a last resort—its throat cut, blood
flowing in a tin plate, foaming, hurried.
Too many spirits to appease! Too much
hunger! Now these mulattos are feeding
on her frail back. Gradually, her head
feels clouded and light, like the curtains
Aséfi made for the house, from old nylon slips.

Caribbean Corpses

Midday. The family sits behind Emmanuel's corpse.
His adolescent granddaughters, self-conscious,
their bursting nipples squeezed in white
Sunday dresses: three child brides for their grandfather's
funeral. Sweat gathers and tickles in the crease
behind their knees. A veil of mosquito netting
is spread over the body in the open casket.
On the wall above the coffin, a porcelain blond
Christ points to his own bleeding heart.

Green mildew lines swerve down Saint Peter's
whitewashed walls in Pétionville. Lizards copulate
behind the old Way of the Cross. One granddaughter
wants to keep this last image of her grandfather:
nose with folded wings which seemed to guard his face;
teeth long and yellowed, some old molars, rotting—
it's almost a relief his lips have now snapped shut.
Her eyes make out his hands—fingers like her father's,

who just happened to cast a glance at his mother
because his ex-wife—number two—is walking up
the aisle, dressed in white lace. Emmanuel's old bride had
already spotted her. Today she must mask
her joy at having won her son back since his divorce.
When she does not nag about his failed marriages
she complains about his now-dead father—she says
Emmanuel still masturbated at eighty-eight and
it's his own fault if he died. *Oui Maman,* her son says;
"The doctor thinks I starved him but it is not so";
Oui M'man; "...couldn't come to the table...has no strength...
a hypochondriac! It's his own damn fault!" *Oui M'man.*

Mosquitoes buzz in circle formation over sweaty scalps
of women smelling of too much Frangipani or Florida Cologne.
Dressed in lace, satin, taffeta, they fan themselves

with one hand, slap flies with the other.
Men, in dark suits, repeatedly wipe their foreheads
and the backs of their necks; so does the government's
representative sent to pay homage to the years
Emmanuel worked as a state civil engineer.
People searching the ceiling for air vents,
wondering who the hell planned this building like that,
find Saint Theresa's eyes are also looking up to
heaven while Saint Lucy carries hers on a plate.

Late, just off a plane from the U.S., Emmanuel's
daughter arrives at the portal. She enters
with a long wail. Her friends turn bored
and bloated eyes from either side of the aisle. She runs
to bury her face in her father's veil. Her mother's jealous
displeasure is distracted by a commotion
in the next chapel where a new widow
screams from the top of her lungs there is black magic
in this place, the Priest is a God-damn-
black-ass-Zombie-maker-husband-thief!
It's the wrong fucking corpse in the box.

Now something new is coming slowly down the aisle:
a white three-legged bitch with yellow eyes,
its head low, tail tucked close between the hind legs,
drooped tits brushing the mosaic floor. It pauses,
looks people briefly in the eyes, finally walks
up to where Emmanuel lies. A breeze almost
lifts the veil but the dog drops a paw on it just
in time, pulls it all off into a pile, thinking
Ha! Human beings and their white veils! Give me a break...
Sits on it, yawns, scratches its fleas with a vengeance.

for Allen Litowitz

Returning Home/Back-a-Yard

Returning home to grade five now
to Mister Blackwood's jockey pointer
and Mistress Sommerville's short fingers—
their long lessons beneath that mammoth

guango tree; to hoppers popping
and squirting from grass—our own green-
and-brown bubbly; and the dominick fowls
coupling nearby. I return now

to our cricket pitch, fresh-pressed
like cloth, and creased with chalk;
and the yellow coconut gravy at noon—
nothing hurried but my face

in curry goat and chicken; and at recess
the draw of darling, knock-kneed Arlene
(and fassy-foot me) to the river—Lawd.
("Yes, Pupa, she married now—

some plantation man from over so.")
In her yard, retraining here,
Mistress Sommerville wells up and
her roosters make roll calls.

Present—I am present.

And Wednesday night's tambourines
at Burnside Church—our elders read
the Bible the way we call out Aesop
in the day, and they sing out Jordan

the way we roll and muddle, "Jamaica,
land we love." And just 'round the corner
Mas' Lickle still a tangle with Mr. Appleton's
bottle and he's losing still—this red man's
folks not sending two pence from Foreign
though everyone else get their barrels.

Returning home, the children stream up
on either side, crumpling starch-pressed
uniforms and giggling, at me, the loved one
they want to touch, who talks like tourists do,
who has lenses to zap their souls, to freeze-
dry and take them back a Foreign.

Returning home, they slant their eyes
away from one too long in the winter,
one too long among the dead.

Poem for Josephine Baker

It flew in through the kitchen window
that summer a few years after the war,
the year I turned four or five,
that fragile yellow bird Made In Japan
whose insides had been sucked out
when the bomb fell on Hiroshima.

All it required for nourishment
was the sweet, cold water
I poured into the slot in its back.

When I blew on the tail feathers,
experimenting with trills, warbling
like some lonely sax man
'round midnight in his sleepless room,
an exile in graceful Paris,
I didn't know then, in that small town,
the other side of the tracks,
I had learned a little, enough
of the secret language of birds.

When that song fluttered into my life again
I knew how to say "Hello. Welcome!" and
"My. It's been a long, long time."

JAN RICHMAN

Driving Out of Providence

I can't see anything at first. My eyeballs are air-drying in the night's fake leather interior. It's like I'm backwards crying, the tears sucked out from behind my eyes into the chamber of my head, sloshing there amongst the already wet deception-sensors and the spongy flowers of incorrect assumptions. But the front slits, the parts that saw you & wanted you, are parchment-dry. Gummy-dry. Amnesia-dry. Suddenly the road jabs its little white stick noodles into my area of expertise. *You will always be hungry,* the white beats say, *but you will not die of hunger. Hunger feeds you.* That's when the radio kicks in and some rough edge writes itself into the smooth concrete of a summer sidewalk, carving deep & spitting out gray peels of what gets left behind. I don't know what to do with all the remainders.

Hours later, my window rolled down, I realize I am on the precise border between away from and toward. And then I've crossed it, despairingly. I stop at McDonald's but the restroom key breaks off in the lock and I pitch the pancake-sized Hamburglar key ring out into the lonely bushes and squat behind a turquoise Tracker in the parking lot, watching my pee collect blackly like oil spill under its wheel.

No amount of coffee can cut through last night's whiskey, but the sun elopes from the water exactly the way I would want to emerge from bad luck, slickly and fatly, like a cell squeezing out of another cell. First you thought I was joking, because you imagine silence as cunning, whereas in my case it's only shrugging, a goodbye waiting to happen. Those few wordless moments are heady, though; they taste like you, like plums & beer.

Preparation for Burial

You've told me how they bury the dead in Ghana—
how they lay each, finally, in the heart of his life:
a twelve-foot wooden cocoa pod or onion for the farmer,
chiefs in slick gold eagles two-men-tall,
and crab, crayfish, lobster, sanded tuna coffins—

because now that you have had me, oh fisherman,
you would like me bellied in a bluefin,
packed in satin and displayed for days, the three days
the soul waits with the body before wandering.

Of course you assume it's you who kept me
alive these months of reeling,
you who shuts my eyes for good,
you who nails on the dorsal fin then over my face
the lid of beautiful blue scales, you who with five men
shoulders my wooden weight and runs me, feet-first,
through every street I've walked.

Three pairs of hands reach for me from the open door of dirt

but this is better than being made-up, laid out
on a bed cornered with obscene red flowers,
better than the procession of drummers
that circled my shade-pulled room,
better than being lip-stitched quiet
while you proclaimed *She is mine, she has always been*
this lovely above the weeping women
who beat a path through the crowd with cloth.

A Story About America

If it is late Sunday in the brain & sunlight
falling on the wall of the Food Court
and you tell me your daughter
at eighteen months still breast-feeds,
and if I with my slightly younger daughter
sitting at the next table nod but say nothing, nothing,
while you speak of the vicissitudes
of cracked-nipples & late-night feedings,
then I am someone who is
you can tell yourself
an odd man, dumb, & probably weird,
weird, weird enough
to see in the baffling dear creature you are
a classical subject for a civilized poet in an innocent land,
such as ours would be.
In that poem you would still be a woman
but made out now as a beautiful thinly-tall broomstick,
pale but not at all bony,
with encircling copper necklace & threaded red sash.

I have a devil, I own a devil,
my devil,
and he'd defend whoever sang.

So all right
I am strange—a usually shameful matter
for an American—and would make myself even more so
to you
by revealing a secret from my life.
It's something.
I watched my wife feed our girl the milk
as both seemed to sleep those minutes
until the baby stopped, started crying,

and I took her downstairs & walked
back & forth on the planked oak floor.
It was 3:31 a.m.,
and I put the music on low
only to initiate my daughter
into the religion of Bob Dylan.
Well I ride on a mail train, baby, can't buy a thrill.
Ain't it just like the night, to play tricks
when you're trying to be so quiet.
I want you to know these things,
and how we did stomp that tune.

So what are you waiting for?

Go ahead, ask.

Don't hold your breath
if you want to breathe,
my beautiful broom.

Angel

Did he save them from the Holocaust to profit his soul, or to make a profit?

Did he make them his slaves to protect them from the Holocaust, or to protect his investment?

"He represented the German system—a guy who could make money."

He made them slaves.

He saved them.

He profited.

Was there any other way he could have saved them?

* * *

Not everyone was saved (not everyone can be saved).

And because not everyone could be saved, the ones who were saved (and their children) were stricken with guilt.

"We the innocent felt guilty what the murderers did to us!"

Some people will do anything to survive.

Who can blame them for wanting to survive?

No day passes when they don't remember—can ever forget—the ones who were lost.

They feel "responsible."

Guilty.

Why should they (and their children) feel so guilty—do they *want* this guilt?

Do we secretly want it for them (and for their children)?

Do we need to cast a shadow?

Don't we suffer enough?

* * *

He was greedy, a womanizer, an adulterer, a drunk—but they questioned only their own morality.

They were slaves in his factory trying to survive a holocaust.

"He provided us with new glasses."

"He delivered our messages."

They called him "Angel."

"We had to accept him as he was.

Nobody else was ready to do as he had done.

He was our Saver!"

* * *

What did it cost him?

He went to prison (briefly), he risked his life (almost) to keep his slaves.

He kept them even when they couldn't work.

Did he understand what he had done?

When the war was over, they saved him from punishment.

He went to South America, tried to start over, but there was no slave labor, and each new business venture failed.

"... the thing that destroyed him as a businessman: common decency."

He died broken; bankrupt; supported by his former slaves; taking a certain moral satisfaction.

* * *

In the movie, the wheeler-dealer, the hard-nosed businessman "with panache," has a sudden change of heart (like Bogart in *Casablanca.*)

He gives up his fortune to keep every slave on his list.

The movie says: *"The list is an absolute good."*

He turns against the Nazis, sabotages their munitions, breaks down and weeps how little he did, how many more he could have saved.

The movie (quoting the Talmud) says: *"Whoever saves one life saves the world entire."*

The movie makes money.

The director wins an award.

"This never would have gotten started," the director says, accepting his award, *"without a survivor ... whom he saved.*

I owe him such a debt—all of us owe him such a debt.

He has carried this story to all of us."

On, Wisconsin

Now they lug in eggplant, zucchini
peppers, honey, apples, cheese
the college jazz band snakes through
slide trombone punching October blue

snare snipping away the seconds.
Above, the golden dome, a manmade sun
and atop, "Wisconsin," a golden woman.
Children roll on the Capitol lawn

leaves litter their clothes, hair
while parents slip loaves and tomatoes
into crowded bags, buy giant cookies
sign petitions for cleaner air,

libertarians, the death penalty.
John McCaffary, 1853,
accused of drowning his wife, Bridget
in a hogshead, the last person

executed in this state, where
today, voices hawk the chair:
"Some crimes deserve the ultimate."
Echoes cajole citizens

in the university's red sweaters
as they purchase preserves, beef jerky.
A pig revolves on a spit, skin
blackened, slick. The mass gawking,

moving in to taste... It was a party
then, too: the juggler with his Empires
his wet, peel-stained smile. The fiddlers,
heads bent forward, together

wheedling their melodies as a child
dances, her hops happily off-beat.
Over two thousand picnickers
fanning themselves in mid-August.

Snap and flutter of the new state's flag
and 31 stars and 13 stripes.
Listen. You can hear traffic on Gorham
honks and curses in the surge to see

young men grope and batter each other
for a pigskin amidst color and cheer.
Listen. The roar of delight
as the body drops, the noose goes taut.

Here is our harvest, on tables, in barrels.
Here are the trappers, the Germans, the Swedes.
Here are the miners, in town for the day.
Here, the hanging tree. Here, the seeds.

Distant Rain

Mama's eyes are turning to clouds,
she forgets the way to the grocery store,
broccoli rots inside the bread box.

Some days she does not know me,
these shoulders she's sponged in the river,
the baby hands she taught to hold water.

Unpinning her cinnamon-roll plaits,
she's chasing light-bugs for diamonds
and playing pity-pat with playmates.

She paces the Trail of Tears with Daddy
strapped to back and seeds of daffodils
neatly folded into the Book of Job.

With full lungs, she pleads save my child
to the fireman who is as yellow as the flames
and turns the water hose on himself.

Lying on back, grayness splattering shoulders,
she whispers of her mother and lilacs,
bed quilted with fading photographs.

But at dawn her eyes rest on the clouds,
emerging spirits pushing up the sun, and she
waves, dividing her face with storms.

And we dance around the tomato garden,
chanting names of old and new friends coming,
like a distant sheet of rain, to take her home.

Motive

for Chris

I'm a penny fallen from heaven's
corner pocket, anybody's overcoat, pick me up
and I'll bring you all kinds of luck. I'm a fence
burning down, love locked in a box, I'm a map

of hand-me-down tomorrows, the last
but one, or anywhere you never wanted
to go, but now. I'm a clock without a face,
I'm blind like time, so lead me on: wear me

on your wrist and I'll tell you things
you might not know, secrets spilled
like a rain forecast. I'm a cup you can
drink me from, cut glass and lucid

distortion, I'm solid water shattering
in hand, or daylight on a midnight
lake. *Remains* is what remains
of this, ambiguous number and tense

as any departure, all impossibility collected
for your sake. Greenhouse, little summer
under winter's latinate lattice of stars,
early or old snow, you're the reason

inside things, sheer likelihood: sense of speed
in the always almost here, the whitedark justice of us.

Squash Flowers

We were both sitting in old-fashioned green metal lawn chairs that rocked back gently on metal tube frames if you wanted them to, and I did. I rocked as I sipped the strong, lemony tea up through the straw, hoping Mrs. Eelpout would tell me a story. She was sniffling, still getting used to the news: Her friend and neighbor's cremated ashes had been found in a garbage can.

Mrs. Eelpout was wearing tortoise-shell glasses that swooped up at the corners, making her look like a lynx. The lenses seemed to be very, very thick bifocals with wavy half-moons across the bottoms for reading. Her hand trembled as she placed her own glass on the wrought-iron table between us. I was afraid she might spill her tea on the tape recorder. It had taken me a while to convince Mrs. Eelpout to let me use it. Only when I'd insisted that nothing was left of poor Mrs. DiLuna, except for a few memories that might be lodged inside Mrs. Eelpout's own head, had she allowed me to switch it on.

"How could someone—her own son, no less—do a thing like that?" Mrs. Eelpout smoothed the apron that she'd put on, for ceremonial purposes, when she went inside the trailer to pour the tea. The apron was clean and pressed, but so worn that the pattern of tiny pink flowers had almost washed away. She'd been shocked at first, then angry, and then weepy when I told her how the new people renting my trailer had found a brass-cornered wooden box in the garbage can out back, containing the cremated remains of her friend.

"Did she ever talk about her last wishes?" I asked. The expression, which I had never used before, felt puckery in my mouth like a bite of grapefruit.

"Sure she did," Mrs. Eelpout said. "She talked about her last wishes, and I talked about mine. She wanted to be buried back East beside her second husband, just like I want to be buried up the hill there in the Abode of Bliss Cemetery, right between my mama and Mr. Eelpout. Why, she had her plot waiting for her, the headstone carved and everything, she told me. Now why couldn't they do that for the poor old thing?"

"Money, probably," I said. "They skipped town after the cremation leaving lots of debts. They never paid the funeral home. They didn't even call an ambulance—they were driving her to the hospital in the next county after she'd had a stroke when she died of congestive heart failure in the back seat—at least that's what the coroner's report says." I leaned forward, checking to make sure the volume on the machine was turned high enough. "And when they got the cremated ashes from the funeral home, they just dumped the box in the garbage can and cleared out, knowing they couldn't pay the bills."

"We were summer friends," Mrs. Eelpout said, shaking her head. "I never stepped foot inside that trailer. Her son's wife, that Sherrie, would help her outside, and she'd settle down right in that very chair you're sitting in. Sherrie'd put an afghan over Mrs. DiLuna's lap, and I'd make some tea, just like now. We'd sit here talking for hours whenever it was fine, listening to the birds, watching things poking up in my little garden. Those were the flowers she loved best." Mrs. Eelpout pointed at some yellow flowers that looked like trumpets, growing up along the edge of the trailer.

"What are they?" I asked.

"Squash flowers—zucchini. But I never get any zucchini. You need the right bee to come along, they say. I wouldn't have bothered with them this year, but I knew Mrs. DiLuna doted on them, and I thought I'd be seeing her again once the weather turned fine. I thought she'd be looking forward to coming outside after being cooped up in that trailer all winter."

"So you didn't visit her in the winter?"

"Once I put on my boots and tramped over—it was before Christmas, and I had a little poinsettia for her—but that woman, that Sherrie, told me she wasn't feeling well. She just took the plant and didn't even invite me in for a moment. I tried calling once, on her birthday in February, but they told me she was too weak to talk on the phone. I knew she was frail. Sometimes when they brought her outside near the end of last summer she was all out of breath. It'd be an hour before she'd be able to say anything."

"Do you think she belonged in a nursing home?"

Mrs. Eelpout sniffed loudly. "I don't wish a nursing home on any poor soul. At least they brought her outside in the fine weather. But not this year. I called to that woman once when she was getting into her car, 'How's his mama?' I called, and she waved, and said, 'She's pretty poorly, the air might be too much for her this summer.' I felt bad. I'd already put in my squash flowers. Then two weeks ago I saw all that trash out front, and the venetian blinds off the windows. I thought they'd just moved in the night, and taken poor Mrs. DiLuna along with them." She lifted the corner of her apron, and dabbed at her eyes. "I had a good cry. Moved away, and we never got to say goodbye. And now this."

The evening sky was a thick egg-white color. The yellow squash flowers were beginning to shrink and close like balloons leaking air. I could almost see them trembling before my eyes. A dove called from the single pine tree that had not been cut down when the trailer court was opened. Back when Denny and I had lived here, before we moved to the new house and began to rent the trailer, we had called it our lonesome pine because we had a view of it from our tiny bedroom window when we made love.

"She was a sweet thing, Minnie was," Mrs. Eelpout said, clearing her throat and looking down at the tape recorder. "We called each other by our first names when we were alone together, you see. She always called me Willa. Willa, she'd say, you do grow the most beautiful zinnias and bachelor buttons. When they first moved in here, it was two summers ago, I couldn't get over the three of them when they got out of the car, that son of hers, Nick, with the ugly wolf tattooed on one shoulder, and that Sherrie, his wife, with her big puffed-up hair, like a high school girl's with a bow on the top, and she almost fifty, and then poor sweet Minnie, her snow-white hair curled like a little lamb's back, trotting behind them with her walker, which they hauled out of the trunk for her. She always had trouble with those steps to the trailer over there—they're not a natural size, I don't think."

I looked over at the trailer. I remembered those steps. I'd even fallen down them once when I'd had too much to drink. Luckily there'd been a deep snowfall, so I'd only landed on my face in a drift. Now I realized we should have called in a carpenter. I hated being a landlady. The only time I'd ever seen Mrs. DiLuna was the time I'd gone over to unstop the sink. Sherrie had leaned against the counter, eating Pringles one by one out of a red can as I worked the plunger, pulling up goop. Afterwards, I'd noticed a mound of blankets on the sofa. It seemed to be moving.

"Nick's mom," Sherrie had said, gesturing with a chip. And I'd seen a tiny little face peeping out at me. I didn't know if she could see me or not, but I smiled. A tiny, crooked hand was clutching the satin edge of one of the blankets.

Denny said he'd seen her a couple of times, when he was over doing repairs. He'd seen her bundled up in a lawn chair one afternoon. We didn't even know her name until the ashes turned up and the sheriff got on the case. I felt especially bad because I wrote about interesting people for the "Life Style" page of our local paper. She hadn't seemed interesting, so I'd ignored her.

But the idea that somebody could end up as ashes in some old battered garbage can really bothered me. My God, she had a life, I told Denny, ninety years of life, and now there's nothing? Is that possible?

He looked at me, nodding wisely, and when I made that little high-pitched shriek he hates so much that I can't help making when something really gets to me, he said, "Why don't you go ask around the trailer court, if that'll make you feel any better?"

"All right, I will," I said. And here I was.

Mrs. Eelpout spread her hands out over her knees and took a deep breath. Her nails were bitten down to the bright pink quick, and it startled me that someone would still be biting her nails in her eighties. I was a nail biter myself, and I kept thinking I'd outgrow the habit. Now I suddenly realized that I never would.

"My memory's not what it was," Mrs. Eelpout said. "We talked about a lot of things, and sometimes we didn't talk at all. But those squash flowers"—she lifted one big hand and waved it over in the direction of the shriveled yellow trumpets—"they'll always remind me of her."

Minnie—her real name in Italian was Dominica, Mrs. Eelpout said—had been taken out of the village school in Sicily when she was nine, and trained to be the cook and housekeeper for the whole family, her father and mother, her seven brothers and sisters, and her grandparents. When they all emigrated to America, she'd been excited, thinking they were going to a place where she'd get to live a real life, like the kind she saw flickering by in the wonderful movies that were shown in the town hall on Sundays after the Angelus. She wanted her lips to be shaped like a bow, and her thick, waist-length hair cut so that it swung against her chin. But nothing changed for her in the new country. Her family lived far out in the sticks, beyond the Baltimore streetcar line; her father beat her and cuffed her just like he had in Sicily, only now there wasn't a village well she could dart down to every day and use as an excuse for exchanging complaints and gossip with other girls and women; and the long cold winter, with its constant rain squalls off the Atlantic and the occasional heavy snowfall, seemed endless.

Gardening was one of her jobs on the farm—in the spring she had to do the hoeing and plant the vegetables and do all the weeding, but she welcomed the work, because it took her away from her father's malevolent reach for most of the day. Suppers were a nightmare. She hadn't cooked the spaghetti al dente, the way he liked it, he said, or else he complained about too much salt in the soup. She usually got a box on the ear, or a slap across the mouth. Later, when she was grown and married, she hated cooking, and all her meals came from Betty Crocker or Kraft.

Once, back in Sicily, she'd planted some lavender and wild carnations in a little plot just for herself. One day her father, tramping about to see if she was keeping after the weeds, had discovered her flowers. His face turned almost maroon. How dare she waste her time on what wasn't edible? He brought shovelfuls of ash from the outdoor oven and dumped them over the bright flowers until they all disappeared into a sooty mound while she stood there watching helplessly, and then he took off his belt and whacked her over the shoulders until she fell face-down in the carrots.

After that, she used to plant row after row of zucchini, because of the yellow flowers. She'd go out into the garden after supper, pretending she was plucking lettuce, and she'd admire their beauty, and when she came back to the house, she kept her eyes lowered so that her father could not see that anything had given her pleasure.

In Maryland, the rich soil felt light and full of air. It did not have the cloying, putrid odor of the Sicilian dirt, turned over every year until it seemed sour, full of rotted tomatoes and moldy, hairy tubers. She dropped her zucchini seeds, a new American variety, into the raked rows, afraid they wouldn't come up for her, but to her joy they sprouted and grew into plants larger than she'd ever seen before. The flowers bloomed, showy as orchids, and she had never seen such firm, perfectly striped zucchini.

She was sixteen. She was assigned to serve dinner to the large table of shouting, drunken men who had gathered to help pick the tomatoes that August. The trestle table was set out under the Concord grape arbor, and she had to go back and forth to the house with platters of spaghetti and big tureens of *puttanesca* sauce. There were jugs of red wine on the table. Some of the older men had faces like twisted pumpkins; the younger men had shiny hair the color of eggplants, and they pinched her bottom when she passed by them if her father wasn't looking. But he was drunk, roaring out jokes and singing snatches from operas. Years afterwards, she'd switch off the radio if she caught even one line of an aria, hating opera as much as she hated the Italian language after she'd learned to speak English.

She'd just returned with another basket of bread when her father's arm lashed out and caught her as if she'd been prey for a crab.

"Here's your wife, Mario," he shouted, pushing her into the arms of a middle-aged man with a thick neck. He was their richest neighbor. His wife had died the year before. She'd seen him looking at her in church.

Now he kissed her so hard that her lips were bruised the next day, shouting as she struggled to get away, "My little anchovy, my little radicchio, I could eat you up!"

"When's the wedding?" somebody shouted.

"Next month she'll be cooking Mario's dinner," her father cackled. "And I'll be admiring my new apple trees."

She knew then that she was being traded for the orchard he coveted, which bordered their own property.

That night she couldn't sleep. She lay very still on her back, her head like a wooden block on the pillow, listening to her sister breathing in the other cot. She decided to kill her father as soon as the house was quiet.

The rifles were kept upright in a rack at the foot of the stairs. She was used to seeing things killed. Her father was always bringing down crows, or lugging bloody rabbits back from the fields. She had seen him put the muzzle of his rifle against the head of an old lame horse that couldn't work anymore, and she had not turned her eyes away at the spewing blood and matter when the bullet exploded. She had helped her brothers push the horse into the pit they had dug down near the creek. Her father had taught her to chop the heads off chickens back in Sicily, guiding her small, horrified hands with his huge, leathery paws.

She knew he had passed out in his favorite chair in the front room. She could hear his rolling snores. Her older brothers were drunk, too, sprawled face-down on the cots in their own room, and her mother was in the bedroom across the hall, the quilt wrapped around her head.

She waited. She felt disembodied, neutral. She had no emotions. There was merely an action to perform, and then she would be free. She knew they would put her in jail, maybe hang her after a trial, but it was better not to try to imagine anything beyond the act she had to perform.

Her sister was breathing gently, her face buried in her hair. She got out of bed so as not to disturb her and quickly dressed in the dark. She looped her high-topped shoes around her neck by their laces and stuffed a pair of cotton stockings into her pocket. Was she going to run away afterwards? Her life seemed like a fantasy to her. She did not know who was in charge, her will or her body.

At the bottom of the stairs, she put her hand on the stock of a rifle. But as she touched the smooth wood, a vibration went through her, as if the gun had just fired, and she had to bite her lip to keep from crying out.

She couldn't kill him. She must have only dreamed that she was going to kill him. She felt clammy and frightened.

A snort, sounding like it came from a mule loose in the house, made her jump back. It was her father. She held her breath until the regular snores resumed.

But the sound brought her back to herself. She couldn't kill him, but she had to do something. She had to get away from this place tonight.

The only place she could think of to go, the only place that in any way belonged to her, besides the bedroom that she shared with her sister, was her garden.

The moonlight shining through the thin clouds seemed especially bright when she stepped outside the kitchen door, careful to make no noise. She could hear the chickens clucking and rustling in the pen. The dog had been tied up in the barn, and his sporadic barks meant nothing. She might be a passing fox or an owl. She found a gunnysack in the shed, then slipped into the garden.

Dew was already coming up from the ground, thick as tears in the grass. Her bare feet were wet. She felt a snail under her toe and drew her foot back before she crushed it. She went down the rows of her zucchini plants and picked every one, no matter the size. She found one last yellow flower still blooming. She hesitated, then put it behind her ear. She heaved the sack over her shoulders.

At the crossroads, she waited for the first wagon to pass on its way to Baltimore with fresh produce. She waved to the man, who pulled up his chuffing team and leaned down, sweeping off his battered felt hat as if to hear her better. She asked him if he wanted to buy some zucchini.

He looked at her curiously, pulling at his mustache. He named a price that was so low that she waved him on, and he shrugged, swirling his whip over his bony horses.

She stopped other wagons. The men were cheeky, and she held herself rigidly, not looking after them as they laughed and pulled away.

An hour later, a young man with distinct, fresh eyebrows, as mobile as caterpillars, agreed to her price. He also agreed to give her a ride into Baltimore and helped her climb up onto the seat beside him. He tossed the sack of zucchini into the back of the wagon, on top of his bushel baskets of tomatoes, and as they clopped slowly toward the city, glowing with new electric lights in the distance, he told her about his sisters, Concetta and Angelica, and how they both worked in the candy factory, where he was sure they could find her a job, too, stirring the vats of chocolate or nougat, or hand-dipping the cherries or nuts, or even placing the cooled candies into the little crinkled papers inside fresh white boxes.

And at night, they would let her bring home the little damaged chocolates to eat herself.

She could go walking to the movies arm in arm with Concetta and Angelica.

On warm nights, she could sit out on the white marble steps and listen to someone down the street play the accordion. Perhaps she would even let him sit beside her, he said softly, and she looked up. Wasn't that star the morning star?

She sat there, looking into the misty distance as she listened to the clop, clop of the horses' hooves carrying her away from a nightmare in which she had almost murdered her father, and into a dream of the future—movies and chocolates and rowhouses with marble steps all mixed together in her sleepy head. A whole long wonderful life stretched ahead of her.

Many years later, married to the man who had helped her escape from home, she'd still sometimes wake with a start in her mortgaged rowhouse beside Memorial Stadium, thinking that she'd just blown her father's head off with a rifle. She'd sit up in bed, clammy in her nightgown, and hug her knees beside her snoring husband, forcing herself to remember how she'd reluctantly gone back to the farm to visit her father on his deathbed. He'd been in a coma, his withered face slack and his breathing raspy. He had not recognized her, but she had knelt at the foot of his four-poster bed along with her frail mother and her spinster sister and her pregnant sisters-in-law, saying the rosary, and she'd wept at his funeral like all the other women. Then, to push away the last cobwebs of the nightmare before she dared to curl back into sleep, she'd remind herself of the moment when she'd lifted her son—the spitting image of his grandfather, according to all the relatives—up to view the coffined face. The boy had struggled in her arms for a moment, not wanting to look, and then at last he'd peeped, frowned, and stuck out his tongue.

Against the Crusades

Don't think that being a left-handed nightingale was all
legerdemain
or that I am that small angry bastard who hates whores,
only I disguised it by laughing; or that it's
easy leaving a restaurant by yourself and holding
your other hand against the bricks to keep from falling;
or anybody can play the harp, or anybody knows the words
to Blue Sunday and After the Ball Was Just Over You Dropped Dead.

If you can stand Strauss then so can I,
O filthy Danube, O filthy Delaware, O filthy Youghiogheny.

And anyone who never opened a Murphy bed
night after night for seven years without ripping
the sheet and had neither desk nor dresser can't walk
in my shoes or wear my crocodile T-shirt.
And anyone thinking that a Jew being a Jew
is something you should apologize for as if Richard
Wagner just stepped into the room wearing a bronze
headpiece with a pink feather sticking out of it
is nothing less than a fool himself who buys into
dead stoves and dead feelings and doesn't know the
sweetness of his own lips and the tenderness of his fingers.

God bless the Jewish comedians who never denigrated blacks,
and God bless the good gentiles and God bless Mayor Scully
and Councilman Wolk and Rosie Rosewall and Eleanor Roosevelt;
and the chorus of Blue Saints behind Bishop Elder Beck
and the old theater on Wylie Avenue I visited every Sunday night
to hear them sing and pray and hear him preach.

God bless the Lucca Café. God bless the green benches
in Father Demo Square and the dear Italian lady
carrying a huge bouquet of red and white roses
in front of her like a candelabra and the tiny white
baby's breath that filled the empty spaces with clapping and singing.

An Explanation

The difference between my house in Pennsylvania
and my house in Massachusetts is the difference between
fish stinking in one place and birds in the other.
The dead and bygone locusts in both places attest to this,
and the salt water bringing the sea back into my inland river.
Suffering being equal, I am happy for the three berries
on the high bush and the mullein sticking out like
swollen asparagus in the sand and grass of Fisher Road.
Basic fruit is what I got, an apple
red as fire on one side, soft and wormy
on the other, something like dew for polish, something
like crapulous breasts, like bulbous bleeding lips.
And eating is what I did, my teeth and tongue
nibbling and sucking as if I were cross-legged still,
as if I had lifted my left hand up and killed
a dragonfly. Both places are edged with phlox
but the water—and the sky—are different. That is why
the currents I moved in were so different and why,
though I started off as one thing, I ended up
as something else. The water took me down
a slice or two. I have become what I was.
Some storm or other changed one thing into another.
You could say that the ocean broke through and what was
fresh water with frogs and lilies and cattails became
much sparser and bleaker, you could say unprotected,
or there was danger and no one knew who had
authority or there was a mix now of salt
and fresh in the mouths of rivers and this was only
transition, and let it go at that. Seen from
above and beyond, out of hearing—and sight—
I could go back *or* forth. Honor and love
to *both* these things. Or I could join one hand
to the other. I used to say "one foot," I said
a river, I said a heart; my brain in the marsh
knows both those things, my freshwater brain, my brain

of pity and fear and cunning, my brain of laughter,
my lung of desperation—sea-water lung—
brackish liver—seaweed stomach—
and skin of pain and skin of adventure and skin
of perfect love and peeling skin and skin of
filth and disgrace, my drum, my lampshade, skin
of water sloshing back and forth, the left hand
brine, the right hand alkaline, the sulphur,
the hard, the soft, the chlorine, the spring, glossy
pokeweed of Millpond Road, long dry grasses of Fisher.

Two Seals

translated by Martha Collins and the author

Are they Julio and Carmen?
Or José and Magreta?
Are they from Ethiopia, or Tanzania?
From the Congo, or somewhere else?

On the beach under the moonlight
They lie side by side
Like two exhausted seals
Thrown from the sea by storm waves.

Their black skin glistens in the moonlight.
They say nothing; they lie together in silence.
Are they listening to the night sea's cry?
Or are they kissing each other,
Or quietly crying?

The sea spray covers them,
Two wet seals that seem to be happy,
That seem to be in pain.
Are they still awake?
Or are they already sleeping
After their long swim?

Wave after white wave breaks on the shore.
Is the sea calling them back
Or pushing them away?

Cuba, 1988

The River Woman's Son

for Margaret

At the edge of a river and the end of a road, a blue-eyed boy lived with his mother and five sisters. The women sewed wedding gowns for every girl from every town. But not one of the river woman's daughters made a dress for herself. They were too plain, too fat, too thin, too tall. A cruel joke, the mother said, because her rosy boy was too pretty for his own good.

The sisters loved him well. They played with him when he was small. Dressed him like a doll in lace and silk. Then one day the river woman caught him pissing in the yard. *Just like your father,* she said, locking the door. From four windows four sisters chanted, *Dirty boys can't sleep in our house.* The youngest sister felt sorry for her little brother and tossed him a plastic bag packed with nuts and bread, three coins, and the boy's go-to-church clothes.

Run away, she whispered, *be like the wind and blow.*

This boy was five years old.

The first day he ate the bread and nuts. The second day he bought tobacco and learned to smoke. On the third day he stuffed his good suit with paper and threw it in the river to watch it float. For a long time he stood on the bank, waving goodbye to his old self.

For weeks, the boy walked town to town, begging quarters, sleeping in barns. Sometimes a kind woman let him wash himself under a hose. One gave him raisins and a cup of broth. One gave him a straw hat to shade his pretty face from the sun. One gave him rope to cinch his pants, which had grown too large and kept falling down. All these women gave their pity, and the pity of women weighed in him like a belly full of stones.

At night they were afraid.

At night they latched their windows tight and bolted all their doors.

Wild boy, face flattened to the glass, he howled. They thought he was the wolf, but he felt the air pass through his hands and the rain wash through his bones. He wanted to tell them, *I'm nothing but a ghost.*

One day, the boy met a man of God. The man said, *I don't have much, but with you, my son, I will share all I own.* The good man's wife washed the filthy boy. Cut his yellow nails. Clipped his matted curls. He saw the ring of scum he left in her porcelain tub, a gray outline of himself. He saw his long locks, coiled like snakes on the bathroom floor.

When the man and wife tucked the boy into his featherbed, they kissed his fingers and his nose. They said, *We love you already. You're our beautiful child now.*

But he was afraid of what he'd lost: ring of silt, sharp nails, twisted curls. He thought these pieces were another boy, still scared and unforgiven, still standing by the river where he'd watched his good self drown.

In the morning, the clean boy discovered that the wife had stayed awake all night to sew him a suit of perfect clothes. The blue shirt was made of silk, the thread of spun gold. The pants were black and tough, the kind that never tore. He told himself he must be good and happy in these clothes.

Still, there was a hole he couldn't fill. His belly was the bear. It growled and growled. Each day he rose hours before dawn to eat alone. He devoured bags of cookies, swilled down quarts of milk. Handful by handful, gulp by gulp, he tried to feed the bear fast enough to keep it still. Soon the skinny boy grew puffed and slow. The too-tight perfect clothes lay folded in a drawer, and the boy wore hand-me-downs. Never again did the good wife wash him, though she complained about his smell.

Then, a miracle! On the church steps the man found a tiny child wrapped in swaddling clothes. This was the true son come at last, the one his wife had waited for.

This baby spoke no words, told no lies, cried hardly at all. This child had no teeth. Every day, a simple girl with swollen breasts came to feed him of herself.

One night the woman whispered to the man, *How can we make the wrong one go?*

Big boy, he frightened them. When he rocked the baby's cradle, he rocked too hard. The woman said, *He has eyes like the coyote. Someday he'll eat my baby whole.*

Her voice was soft, but these words slipped under the door and down the hall; they whirled into the boy's ear, hissing in his skull. His chest burned, full of live coals. He wanted to smash a window, throw the baby out. His hands twitched. His hands said, *Now.* He clasped them tight to make them stop. He wasn't a bad boy. His heart was bright and hot but still a human heart. He saw what the man and wife did not: the baby's head was big, but the baby's brain too small.

He couldn't sleep another night in that bed soft as a cloud. The man of God kept a gun in the closet. The good wife kept a carving knife in the kitchen drawer. The gun told the boy, *I love noise.* The knife said, *I love your throat.*

Before he left, the boy turned every picture to the wall. Since it was almost winter, he stole a pair of leather boots with leather soles, a down jacket, a wool scarf. He stole the precious letters the man and wife kept sealed in a secret box. That night he burned them in a vacant lot. That night he warmed his hands as he watched the words of love go up in smoke. When he poked the cinders with a stick, they crumbled like his heart of coal.

Now the boy was ten years old.

He slept in the woods, curled in a hollow in the ground. Pines swayed. Their highest limbs were strung with stars. Sticks and rocks tore his jacket. All the feathers floated out. Day by day his body consumed itself. He became a scavenger, eater of fish heads and beetles, pig ears and chicken hearts—anything he could catch, anything people who were still people threw out. As his flesh shrank tight, he saw how his pelvis curved. When he touched his tiny ribs, he wanted to snap each bone.

The bear in the belly made the boy break glass and walk through walls. Everything he stole, he lost. The woods were full of children, thieves like him, little wolves. He covered himself with leaves and dirt. He was always cold. Sometimes the leaves pretended to be hands fondling him in the dark.

One evening at dusk, a strange, pale child appeared in the woods. His coat was covered with stiff white hairs, his face with white down. He went from tree to tree and hole to hole, telling all the missing ones that he knew a woman who would let them sleep by her little fire, safe in her little house. But nobody believed him. They disguised themselves as roots and stones.

Buried in the dirt, the boy thought, Maybe this stranger has a slender knife inside his coat. Maybe he's come to kill me for my leather boots though the leather soles are thin as paper now. Then he saw that the pale creature was not a human boy at all. He was a white deer bounding through the trees, leaving only tracks in snow.

The boy followed. When it grew too dark to see, he crawled. At last he saw a candle flickering in a tarpaper shack at the edge of town. Inside, a hunched woman with yellowish skin fed sticks to a pot-bellied stove. He knocked at the window and she opened her door. She wasn't afraid; she didn't scold. When he tore half the bread from the loaf, she offered butter and jam. She said, *Eat all you want, there's more.*

The woman with olive skin was very ugly and very old.

He knew the story of the gingerbread house. So what, he thought, let her fatten me up. When she asks to feel my fingers, I'll give her chicken bones.

But she wasn't that witch. She taught him how to talk again, how to use a knife and fork. She tried to teach him words on the page, but they swirled in his head like wind-whipped snow. They buzzed and cursed. Books made the boy so furious, he ripped the pages out. Sometimes he fed them to the pot-bellied stove. Sometimes he ate them himself.

If he raged enough by day, by night he might grow calm. The clean sheets of his tiny bed were cool against his skin and smooth as silk. They made him remember a blue shirt from long ago. They made him remember piles of wedding clothes. Sometimes they woke him to remind him of his filth. Nights like those, he sat in the tub for hours, scratching at his skin until he had no smell.

The woman kept a jar of coins in the cupboard. Each month she'd go to town. On the day the boy turned sixteen, she told him she'd spent their last coin. He found a job repairing roads. The old woman said he was the man of the house. But curled in his little bed, the boy heard a wailing sound, a child far away, the baby with the brain too small, or just his long-lost self. If he cried too hard, his real mother came, the first one, the one who kicked him out. He dreamed himself delicate as a doll in frilly clothes. Mother's big hands gripped like claws. Mother shook his shoulders till his silly whimpering stopped.

Every morning he forgot. But once he knocked the old woman against a wall, called her an ugly witch, told her he hated her as much as he hated everyone else. Afterward he laid his head in her lap and sobbed. She forgave him, of course. She loved him more than she loved herself.

For her sake, the boy worked hard, though he despised the sticky heat and smell of tar. Dizzy one day, he leaned against his shovel and saw a watery mirage, a swarm of white locusts, thousands of tiny winged women dressed in wedding gowns. The foreman never had liked this boy. The foreman said, *You're fired. You work too goddamn slow.* Later the boy couldn't recall how the other man ended up in the gravel. He didn't remember a silver knife slitting the man's shirt. Didn't hear the knife say, *I could open your bowels.*

All night the boy lay shivering, wrapped in a wool blanket and dressed in all his clothes. The old woman said, *They could send you to prison, you know.*

He hid in the forest. He thought, I can't hurt anyone if I'm alone. But the woman followed him. The woman begged him to come home. She said, *I'll take care of you forever. I can't bear to be alone.*

Strong as a man, this boy stayed a child in the woman's house. She was an old old woman now. She took a job scrubbing toilets and floors. Each day she looked more like a witch. Her hair grew coarse as wires. Her dark teeth fell out.

The boy told himself she was a beautiful princess snared by a wicked charm. If he could break the spell, she'd be a lovely girl. The magic jar would fill itself with gold. One night she drank sweet wine till she passed out. Like a lover, the boy closed his eyes and kissed her wrinkled mouth. But the old drunken woman with seven teeth refused to be transformed.

He loathed her then, her shriveled breasts, her brittle bones. He slapped her face until she woke. He said, *Why did you save me for this?* He said, *When you die, I'll be the one alone.*

She said, *You remind me of myself.* She said, *I was hungry all my life, and cold.*

They wept together then. They drank till they were blind. They laughed and swore. All the glasses jumped from the shelves. All the bottles shattered on the floor. The boy and the old woman kissed each other's mouths. The old woman and her only love fell asleep in each other's arms.

Why do I tell this story?

The boy was my lover, if you want to know. The woman died, and the boy followed me until I took him home. He told me this story. I believed his sorrow and his hunger made him more human and more whole. Vain fool, I thought I could love him as the woman loved. I spoke her words. I said, *You remind me of myself.*

But I lied. I knew nothing of their world. I've starved myself, but I never had to starve. Once on a mountain and once in an ocean, I nearly froze. But I never slept night after night in a hole. On playgrounds and in fields I tackled little boys and pinned them to the ground. It's true. Once I slammed a two-hundred-ten-pound man against a wall. With my fingernails and teeth I've drawn blood from my sister's arms. But I have never held the cold blade to another's flesh and heard the knife say, *I could open your bowels.*

One night we fought. It doesn't matter why. Some silly thing. I don't remember now.

Later, he thought I was asleep and touched me in the dark. This terrified me more than anything else. More than curses on the stairs, clenched fists, the threat of broken bones. His hands were cool as metal between my thighs. He whispered that he loved me, but I heard other words hammering in my skull. His fingers spoke. They said, *We could kill you now.* The sharp edges of his hands slipped inside my body. They said, *We could scoop you out.* In absolute silence his veins said, *Washed in your warm blood, we will be clean. Darling,* they said, *with your bright blood at last we will be filled.*

Westbound

First a startle of fragrances
to remind me where I am:
turf smoke blown through drizzle,
oystery brine-tang over Quay Street.

An umbrella-raking gale.
Then mind-blowing blue above the town for a nanosecond
    until my airport-bound rented windscreen
        spatters with the weather's wet
       splash of anticipation and
by an astral lope I'm back in a place with trees where

I picture you holding open a Victorian door shyly—
    then an almost imperceptible bouquet
       of lavender and myrrh
      from between your thighs.

Two virtues of a Catholic girlhood:
the name Mary, and secrets in the dark.

 This far away I can touch the hard nubby stars
of chrysanthemums that I put in the ground,
    watered and husbanded. They bud up now.

          Petit Sirah
and, as a present for you, note cards
    with Kilkenny rooks
        settling among smoky chimney stacks and copper beeches.

But how can I write on flat paper
this impulse that arcs between us, inarticulately,
      as I fly?

from *Rosary*

Do I begin at the here and now,
or does the story start
with the first time
my mother took the wheel—
the first woman to drive
in a country where men
are afraid to walk?

My mother's story begins
when the steam rises.
It ends when it's ready.
Taste it. Does it need more salt?

Heat

Today, at sixty-seven, she stands at the stove at work. The heat overcomes her. She thinks she is standing at the shore. The steam is like a warm breeze being carried out to sea. My mother hears the seagulls circling above. She feels the sun on her skin and admires the reflection on all the shining fish bodies. Her father's men have been collecting the nets for days now, laying the fish out for fermenting. The gull with the pure white underside swoops toward the fish farthest away, lands on an overturned boat, its sides beaten and worn, its bottom sunburned like a toddler's face after her first day of work in the rice fields. Beside the boat, a palm hut, where the fishermen hang their shirts, and where their wives change when it's time for a break from the scooping and jarring, when their black pants become hot as the sand itself. And then the laughter starts, and the women's bodies uncurl from their stooped positions, their pointed hats falling back, the men treading anxiously in the water as they imagine a ribbon pulling gently at each soft chin.

Bait

Through the eye, my grandfather threads the rusty hook, forces it back through the body of the fish. The tail curves around as if frozen mid-leap. The seagulls never leave. The smell of fish always in the air. Today, the old man will give them nothing. It is his daughter he is thinking of. My mother is fourteen and beginning to turn heads. Her father thinks she will like the seagull with the pure white underside. He watches the birds, daring one another to come closer. He watches the younger ones in their confusion. The swoop and retreat. He has not fed them for days. Minutes go by, and he thinks the boats will come in soon, scattering the gulls. The Year of the Snake is only days away. He would buy his daughter a dove, but she likes the wind. With a quick swoop, a gull grabs the fish in its beak. The old man wraps the line around his roughened hands, braces himself for the tug, as the line grows more taut. And suddenly the bird jerks in the sky, wings extended as if it's been shot.

Cage

Easter lilies spill from her thin arms. The flowers and her gloves equally as spotless. This is how it began. My mother would never forget the seagull with the hook through its bill. Often she would recall how wrong the imagination could go. All she had been thinking about was the pure white of its underside. Not the high-pitched cry of a child being separated from all it knows. The best part was seeing it finally take to its wings again. It was still in the cage that her father had built, but she could pretend it had its freedom. It could fly higher than she could reach.

Downpour

She knew it was coming by the way the glass jars shook in the darkness, the occasional flash of lightning, crawling the walls like quick lizards. A rain so heavy, things would be hammered into the earth. She thought of all the glass jars resting on their shelves, all the hours the men spent, blowing these cylinders for the *nuoc mam* they made from the anchovies they caught, and then, the few drinking glasses they made for themselves on the side when her father wasn't watching. After the rain, the broken pieces would once again have to be melted down and mixed together. And here, her father lay in bed, smoking away the profits. With each breath in, the fishing boats moved farther and farther away. With each breath out, more jars needed to be made, sold. Her father couldn't even hear the thunder. The lightning, warm flashes on his lids, like the sun when he was trying to nap in the afternoon. He thought the glass-blowers earned him a puff on his pipe with each puff on theirs. He should reap the rewards of being an old man, of owning his own fishery. But with each breath, his daughter grows more impossibly beautiful. He knows he will not be able to keep her long.

Safe

The three sisters watch her lean over as they sip their tea, as they try to keep up the conversation, try not to alert her that they are watching as she uncovers the safe, piles the bars of gold to the side, and pulls out the sack of bills, grabbing two bundles and putting the rest back. She covers the safe with the red cloth as before, bowing to the picture of her grandmother. The women think of their brother in Saigon, playing poker in his white jacket, his slicked back hair. They think of the young girls he has loved, the ones he has impregnated, they think of all the angry parents they have faced. Then they think of him married, married to Tran Thi Marie, driving her father's Mercedes; they remember her grandfather and his plot full of banana trees and fruit drying in the sun; they have seen her father's fishing fleet. They think of all the delicious meals they will enjoy when they visit their brother. Marie is a gorgeous woman. They will tell their mother.

Faith

For years, my grandfather thought he could keep my mother by his side. She seemed content with her prayers and fasting. But he didn't know about the couple that sat before her at Mass that Sunday morning. She had noticed them, the man sitting next to the woman as if she were any other. But then, the stolen glances, the passing of a prayer book, the spreading of goose bumps, from the neck down the arms, the woman crossing herself.

The first time my father saw my mother, she was driving the barren countryside of Bien Ho. How vain, he thought to himself: wearing Easter lilies in her hair. What he didn't know was that they actually were Easter lilies, she was on her way to Mass. She wore them year-round to remind herself that Jesus was always risen—if you kept Him alive in your life.

Proof

They were married before her father knew it,
her father smoking opium in the bright sun.
All he could remember
was the white jacket, the black tie,
the boat rocking, the boys reaching,
dragging the net.
The net full of fish.
The fish drying in the sun.
The seagulls swarming like men
honing in on the scent.
The slow peeling of an orange.
Smoke coming from his pipe.
The juice squirting.
The spewing out of pits.
And then, she was packing.

Prayer

My grandfather had always had three women in the kitchen, someone continuously preparing something. Fresh bread, hot banana pudding, sweet rice with coconut. And now his daughter was leaving, and the women were selecting china for her to take. He wondered how this happened. She was the last of his daughters, and he had spoiled her, hoping to keep her for himself. For years, he spent his days, from the moment he woke until the sun began its slow dive into the water, submerged, working the fishing nets, his skin puckered like a mango left in the sun too long. And here, his daughter would still need to watch the gills heave up and down, the gasping at the small mouth. Still, she'd need to chop the head off, blood running down the sides of the cutting board, her hands covered with scales. For years, he tried to keep her hands from coming in contact with anything but the food she ate and the money she counted. Now they would be roasted daily over a fire.

He wondered how crowded her new home would be, how long she would have to live with her in-laws, how such a small child would bear a child. He knew she would find it difficult to breathe in the smog-filled streets of Saigon. He closed the trunk for her, knelt down beside her, pressed a bar of gold into her palm. He wanted her to write as often as possible. She nodded. She wanted to stay, to hold her father's hand, to watch the fishing boats come in, to listen to the seagulls like hungry beggars outside.

Hope

It all began with her driving the barren country roads, barren because the men were too fearful to walk them. Knife blade to the neck, my mother still refused to hand over the pearls her father gave her for her first Christmas as a teen, as a target for unmarried men. Really, what she hoped they wouldn't find was the pearl rosary her mother left behind. She felt the blade bite deeper into her neck: the same place her husband would often bite her the first year they were married, the last year she would think of love as something shared between two people.

After the first child, she would think of duty and responsibility and mirrors. She cared for herself and so, her child. Love remained between her and God. Husbands were meant to be fathers, children to be married off. Her mother's rosary was proof she agreed. The cross was melded from her wedding ring. It was crooked from being slammed in the door as she ran from her husband. One day my mother would hide the same beads beneath her pillow, as if to ward her own husband away, as if after seven children, he might somehow stop.

Hunger

In Saigon, a daughter on each hip, she began to wonder where the rice was going. Leaving one child home sucking her thumb, the other holding her empty belly, my mother hailed a taxi. In front of the cathedral, the pink nails in the car ahead crept across the man's neck, and she recognized both. This was, after all, the man who woke her body. Before him, she knew only the ache of chopping and carrying, of balancing heavy loads. Now there was a different kind of pull, like the sea, and after it, a different kind of heavy load, filling her belly. Of course, she followed him.

*   *   *

Balance

On the way back from the market each day, the pole teeters across her back, a pot on either side. The one on the right, emptied of its *pho;* the one on the left, full of dirty bowls and the leftover dishwater she was too impatient to drain. Cuong skips ahead, his short hair bouncing with each step. She quickens and grabs her youngest son's ear, twisting it, not because he is getting too far ahead, or because he is daydreaming, but because she can't. Her husband gone with the two oldest children, my mother still has four. He lives in a duplex in Manhattan; she sells *pho* for ten cents a bowl and needs someone to hold. Cuong is getting too big, with his slingshots and firecrackers, his patched eye from Tet. Each day she drags my grandmother's bed a little closer to hers, brings a mirror along with dinner to her mother's bedside.

Measure

My mother's recipes are not even close to precise. Everything is in approximate proportion. One portion of *nuoc mam* to three of water and one of vinegar, some lime, a big pour of sugar. Maybe some more. This is in opposition to her determination to keep my father. With this, she was painfully methodical.

When she got off the plane, rosary wound around her left hand, her right dragging Cuong along, did she think about the child growing inside her? I was not yet growing inside her, but she knew I would be soon. She knew also that there was a child growing inside some other woman's womb, and that it would be born first, and that her husband would be there. Still, she had four children in tow, all of whom would cry out *"Ba!"* on cue. They had had enough rice with *canh* for dinner. Now they were in the United States of America, with all its independence and escalators, its planes, trains, and fast ways of getting away. They weren't letting go.

Epilogue

Brush stroke number 49
and her hair shines like a black cat's.
She can think of nothing
but the days when she wore her hair
above her shoulders, moved her hips
like a boy. And still the men
couldn't help but look. Now
there are so many things
to fit into the frying pan:
the daughter with the red
lingerie rolled inside her dirty
school uniform, the son
with the twisted jaw
and the constant longing
for a cold beer, the husband
she chased in taxicabs,
holding her extended belly
only to finally say, *Please,*
take me home. At seventeen,
my mother counted her Hail Marys
on the little white beads
of her rosary. Now she counts them off
on the heads of her seven children,
counting herself as eight,
and her husband,
as one and ten.

JON TRIBBLE

Tail Dragger

Ain't no way this river or any other
is wide enough to slow us down, no
bust-gut half-ass ocean got the means
nor the notion to make this anything
but fine—
              why bother to slip on or out
of that little bit of nevermind tonight
cause it don't matter none to rhythm
and blues we're percolating here and
now forever till tomorrow—
                          it's too
damn easy to realize the syncopation
of my hand your thigh your mouth my
back and over and over till we find
the music in the motion winding on
to this moonlight fever—
                          and we burn
like acetylene lighting steel like rhyme
fighting reason making too good for
somethings into an ecstatic spark opening
the wicked licks of a heavenly axe.

From the Postcard at Vertigo Bookstore in D.C.

In the photograph of Billie Holiday taken by Mickey Pallas at the 1957 Newport Jazz Festival, she wears a low-cut evening gown & a fawn-colored stole. Her rhinestone earrings are shoulder-dusters, & her necklace falls almost to her cleavage in heavy leaves of glass stones, or maybe they are real (though paste gems on Billie Holiday never subtracted from her quality). The bracelet on her large wrist spans wide as a man's shirt cuff, & her nails are frosted. The cigarette comes out at you, foreshortened over a score where the notes are few with wide spaces between . . . Her hairline is even as Nefertiti's, eyebrows painted on in thick confidence, & her lips, most likely red, are round in generous laughter for the photographer it seems. She is not performing: that was before, or she's going on later. Billie Holiday is chic on her break; & when women open their little drawers of half-used lipsticks two shades off, & mascaras bought in anticipation of an event like the Newport Jazz Festival, they know as I do looking at my stash of packaged glamour—we look for it, & it's not there.

Wedding Dress

She wants it and she doesn't want it: the lace neck
and sleeves, the waist so tight she'll need it refitted
the day before *the* day. She wants and doesn't want
the pleats and puffs and bows, the veil's force field
guarding her face, the train's long barge dragging behind,
the whole creation so elaborate she must be lowered
into it—like a knight onto his horse—with a crane.

She wants and doesn't want to choose her neckline:
Bateau, Bertha, jewel, Queen Anne, décolletage;
her sleeves: *bishop, balloon, pouf, gauntlet, mutton-leg;*
her silhouette: *ball gown, basque, empire, sheath, mermaid;*
her headpiece: *pillbox, derby, wreath, tiara, garden hat.*
She wants and doesn't want the four-page guest list,
the country club that overlooks the valley

like an Indian tribe planning surprise attack.
She wants and doesn't want the triptych invitations,
the florist/psychic who intones, "I envision one black
vase per table, each holding a single white rose."
"I love him," she thinks, "but my Zeppelin tapes are melting;
my Bowie posters curling into flame. I love him,
but Uni High is vanishing like our senior *Brigadoon.*

I love him but my friends are turning into toasters,
china place settings, crystal salad bowls." She wants
and doesn't want the plane door closing,
Tahiti rushing toward her, then dropping behind,
Mom in her fuchsia gown starting to stoop,
Dad giving her away as white hair falls: a fairy ring
around his feet. Even as she pays for it, her dress

is yellowing, the wedding pictures aging into artifacts,
her children staring at strangers: one in a penguin suit,
one in her glory. They can't believe that living
works this way—just as the boy can't believe what else
his pecker will be for; the girl, where babies grow,
how they get there, what every month will leak from her.
I want it, but I don't want it, she'll say.

DAVID WOJAHN

Red Ochre

Ozone smell: all afternoon
    the rain turned off and on like spray
        slurring out a tap. She's floating along

the fern bar window, and the couples
    scoring paper tablecloths with crayons,
        circles and arrows as they laugh,

cigarette-glow and darting eyes, margaritas
    all around, salt crust on the glass rims.
        Then she's passed their tinted pane,

sidewalk pocked with drizzle, glazing
    while she kills time, waiting to call
        for the test results. She conjures

the lab, the centrifuges' hiss
    and whirl, specimens and samples
        towering in a room her mind makes

long and narrow as the university
    pool she's walking from, and its air
        as thickly humid. Her sari

billows in the wind and spotty rain.
    She's thinking to think
        away: cedar waxwing, goldfinch,

tarpit, a spike of red ochre
    with one side sharpened—
        a writing stick from Pleistocene

Australia, unearthed in this morning's
    section three. And the fifty-two sons
        of Rameses: someone's cleaning rubble

from all the basalt sarcophagi.
    Think away to her thirty-fourth lap,
        her goggles unfogging and then

the good air swallowed,
    great draughts at the poolside,
        great tectonic draughts.

Chlorine sting, the nostrils
    flaring and her own slick palm
        inching her neck to reckon the pulse.

LISA YANOVER

In the Pardes

It is still dark when the trucks take us to work in the citrus groves,
when we pull on our gloves and climb ladders into the trees.
In the morning dark, workers go without faces. They are trunks
and limbs like the trees they inhabit. I am counting the people
like trees, counting in Hebrew the oranges dropping into the crate.
Every twelve or so oranges, I lose count and begin again.
I tell myself I am counting Jews. Another Jew drops
into the crate. Perhaps he is on his way to Europe: to Poland
or Czernowitz. Perhaps he will visit my relatives in Russia,
if I have relatives in Russia still living. Or perhaps he will visit
the dead, place stones by their graves in the Jewish cemetery,
if the Jewish cemetery is still standing. The Russians
do not mind the Jewish dead and leave them alone. Perhaps
he will follow my grandparents west to America, shouting
from the rails of the ship, from the dark below, "Thank God
    for Columbus!"
Perhaps his children's shouts, like my parents', will be practical,
less ecstatic—and I, if I shout at all, shout inwardly, guiltily.
In the shrinking dark, this Jew I am holding, this Jew I send
into exile seems to be smiling. Perhaps he envisions his return,
not the tedious flight of this generation, passports, customs,
security checks, but the night rush of immigrants, waiting offshore
for the light in the window, the newcomers carried to land,
the landowner and his family shoving oranges into their hands
and pockets as they run to meet loved ones, as they run
into the dark of the citrus groves toward us.

Celebration of the Body

translated by George Evans and the author

I love this body that's lived through life,
its amphora shape, its water smoothness,
its streaming hair that crowns the skull,
the delicate stem of its crystal face
ascending exquisitely from shoulders and collarbones.

I love my back sprayed with muted bright stars,
my translucent hills, wellsprings of the breast
that provide primary sustenance to the species.
Cliff-like rib cage, waist in motion,
my womb a warm, overflowing vessel.

I love the moon-like curve of my hips
shaped by successive births,
the sharp curving wave of my ass;
and my legs and feet, foundation and support for the temple.

I love its handful of dark petals, its hidden fleece
that guards the mysterious entrance to paradise,
the damp cave from which blood flows
and birth-water springs.

This suffering body of mine that gets sick,
that leaks, that coughs, that sweats,
secretes humors and feces and spit,
gets tired, worn out, fades away.

Living body, a link that insures
an infinite chain of successive bodies.
I love this body made of the richest mud:
seeds, roots, sap, flowers and fruit.

ABOUT YUSEF KOMUNYAKAA

A Profile by Susan Conley

Yusef Komunyakaa speaks in a gravelly Southern baritone, tinged with a Cajun flavor that reflects his childhood years in Louisiana. He is a man who chooses his words carefully, splicing his speech with long silences, until his conversation resembles something close to a jazz riff—very fitting for this acclaimed poet who says "oral language is our first music, and the body is an amplifier."

Music, more specifically radio music, playing from a waist-high, wooden radio in his mother's living room, was Komunyakaa's first link to the world outside his hometown of Bogalusa, Louisiana. Born in 1947, Komunyakaa grew to revere the radio, and it became a shrine for him: he would listen to Louis Armstrong, Dinah Washington, and Mahalia Jackson and feel a connection to something larger than the rituals of sports and hunting in his own rural town. The jazz and blues Komunyakaa heard as a child have gone on to inform much of his nine published books of poetry. Not afraid to confront complex moral issues, much of Komunyakaa's work embraces the duality of despair and hope, and music often provides the panacea. All kinds of musicians show up to play: Otis Redding, John Coltrane, Ray Charles, Charles Mingus, and Thelonius Monk, to name a few. The result is a celebration of African American heritage and culture.

In 1994 Komunyakaa received the Pulitzer Prize, the Kingsley Tufts Award, and the William Faulkner Prize from Université de Rennes for *Neon Vernacular: New and Selected Poems,* a collection that prompted many to deem him the progenitor of a wholly new poetic vernacular. Fiercely autobiographical, the spare poems in the book deftly interweave surrealistic imagery, montage, and folk idiom. They offer detailed glimpses of Komunyakaa's rural upbringing, his identity as an African American, as well as his experience in the jungles of Vietnam. Komunyakaa's lines are consistently short and unrhymed, strung together with conso-

Photo: Mandy Sayer

nance to arrive at a unique syncopation. The compression and jazz-inspired enjambment create a music-like tension:

> Heat lightning jumpstarts the slow
> afternoon & a syncopated rainfall
> peppers the tinroof like Philly Joe
> Jones' brushes reaching for a dusky
> backbeat across the high hat. Rhythm
> like cells multiplying...language &
> notes made flesh. Accents & stresses,
> almost sexual. Pleasure's knot; to wrestle
> the mind down to unrelenting white space,
> to fill each room with spring's contagious
> changes. Words & Music...
>
> —from "Changes"

Growing up in Bogalusa in the 1950's was not easy for Komunyakaa. He describes it as "a typical Southern town: one paper mill that dominated the place, and a public library that did not admit blacks." The oldest of six children, his relationship with his father became "a kind of contest early on"—one which Komunyakaa worked hard to win. His father, a carpenter, adhered to a "black Calvinist illusion that menial labor could lead to great heights."

Komunyakaa took two after-school jobs on the side and spent most of his hours "in far-off mental landscapes" trying to "daydream myself away from the place."

In retrospect, he supposes daydreaming, as well as being a coping mechanism, was his first important creative act—one that may have kept him alive. Bogalusa was the backdrop for an active Ku Klux Klan. In "Fog Galleon," Komunyakaa writes: "I press against the taxicab / Window. I'm back here, interfaced / With a dead phosphorescence; / The whole town smells / Like the world's oldest anger." Komunyakaa considers a James Baldwin quote about racism as a perfect mirror to his own childhood: "if a black boy, by the time he's fourteen years old, doesn't know the score, there's no way he can survive."

The only problem, as Komunyakaa sees it, is that he never really learned the score. He never knew how precarious his life was in Louisiana—a place where race was "too important, and caused so much tension," a place where you sat "in the back of the bus, and there wasn't a black policeman." His grandmothers, with whom he has remained very close, tried to explain "the dos and the don'ts" of life in the South. They also stressed to him the importance of his family name. People have often assumed Komunyakaa's name implies he is Muslim, and during the 1970's, he did nothing to dispel the notion. He was drawn to the religion and read its literature. However, the name was actually brought to America by Komunyakaa's grandfather, a stowaway, on a ship from Trinidad.

The first book Komunyakaa found time to read as a boy was the Bible—which he read twice in its entirety. He cannot underestimate its effect on his own writing: "The hypnotic Biblical cadence brought me close to the texture of language, to the importance of music and metaphor." After Poe, Tennyson, Shakespeare, the Harlem Renaissance writers, and Gwendolyn Brooks, he also got his hands on works by James Baldwin, and even wrote a poem for his graduating high school class: one hundred lines in rhyme.

Komunyakaa left Bogalusa briefly for Phoenix and then Puerto Rico, but within a couple of years, after basic training and Infantry OCS, he was on an airplane to Vietnam, where he served as an information specialist and later an editor for the military newspaper *The Southern Cross.* Politically against the war and its senseless violence, Komunyakaa had thought of going AWOL. However, the idea of "bearing witness" lured him. Once he arrived, "the pressures of survival were so woven into who I was, into who we are as humans, that if placed against a war, one reacts to survive." Only in retrospect did Komunyakaa realize how dangerous his tour in Vietnam was: "Every time anything happened within the area of operation, I found myself on a chopper, out to the action."

Before returning home Komunyakaa received the Bronze Star for his duty in Vietnam. However, he preferred not to talk about the war with anyone. He enrolled in the University of Colorado in 1973 and took a creative writing class with Dr. Alex Blackburn; he has been writing ever since. After a double-major in English and sociology, and a last-minute decision not to pursue a Ph.D. in psychology, Komunyakaa went on to get an M.A. in creative writing from Colorado State. At this point, Komunyakaa knew he needed more time to hone his craft and headed to the University of California, Irvine, to pursue an M.F.A. During this time he read widely: T. S. Eliot, Ezra Pound, Paul Celan, Aimé Césaire, Baudelaire, the French Surrealists, Jean Toomer, Robert Hayden, Bob Kaufman, Helene Johnson, and Amiri Baraka. He also kept developing his musical ear—listening to what he calls "world music": jazz, blues, classical, Latin, as well as others.

He published his first chapbook, *Dedications and Other Dark Horses*, in 1977 and his second, *Lost in the Bonewheel Factory*, in 1979. By 1981 Komunyakaa had received fellowships from the Fine Arts Work Center in Provincetown and the National Endowment for the Arts. His next book, *Copacetic,* an evocative collection of jazz-inspired poems examining his childhood, came out with Wesleyan University Press in 1984 and gained resounding praise from reviewers. His fourth volume, *I Apologize for the Eyes in My Head*, which followed in 1986, began to tap into the violence of Vietnam: "I am a man. I've scuffed / in mudholes, broken teeth in a grinning skull / like the moon behind bars" (from "Unnatural State of the Unicorn"). The book gained national attention and won the San Francisco Poetry Center Award, but it was not until *Dien Cai Dau* in 1988 that Komunyakaa gained full access to his Vietnam experiences.

Dien Cai Dau, which means "crazy" in Vietnamese, stands as a watershed. Fourteen years after returning from Vietnam, instead of merely "writing around the war," Komunyakaa finally "uncapped a hidden place" inside himself. "I tend to tell people that we are walking reservoirs of images. We take in everything, even what we're not overly conscious of, it's still there, pulsating in the psyche." Komunyakaa was standing on a ladder, renovating his house in New Orleans, when poems about Vietnam started spilling out. *The Village Voice* wrote that *Dien Cai Dau* "drove a shaft of light into the inarticulate spectacle of the Vietnam War." The poems grapple with the numbing violence of the war and with the frustrations of black soldiers in predominantly white platoons. Empathy with the enemy is also explored, as in "Starlight Scope Myopia," where the speaker of the poem looks to the other side: "...Caught in the infrared / what are they saying? / / Are they talking about women / or calling the Americans / /*beaucoup dien cai dau*? / One of them is laughing. / You want to place a finger / / to his lips & say 'Shhhh.'..."

In *Magic City*, published in 1992 by Wesleyan, Komunyakaa turned back to his youth, revisiting it with an unflinching eye. The result is poetry that refuses to offer a simple reprieve for our history of racism, poetry that insists we pay witness to life in all its contradictions. At times, these poems are achingly personal, as in "My Father's Love Letters," where the speaker must transcribe letters to his mother for his illiterate father: "On Fridays he'd open a can of Jax / After coming home from the mill, / & ask me to write a letter to my mother / Who sends postcards of desert flowers / Taller than men. He would beg, / Promising to never beat her / Again..."

In 1982 Komunyakaa began teaching at the University of New Orleans. He also worked as a visiting poet for the public school system, teaching enthusiastic fourth and fifth graders that poetry "is a sharing of feelings and ideas." It was in New Orleans that he met his future wife, Australian fiction writer Mandy Sayer. They then moved in 1985 to Bloomington, where he was a professor of English at Indiana University until 1996. Recently, his life has been considerably more peripatetic. He completed a year-long stint as the Holloway Lecturer at the University of California, Berkeley, and is now on a one-year stopover at Washington University in St. Louis before a permanent position at Princeton University begins next year.

Komunyakaa is not choosy about when he lets his muse descend; he often has enough subject matter to work on three collections simultaneously. He prefers to write every day. He finds the early morning full of "very surprising moments," and jots down notes on a pad beside his bed upon waking. His method is inclusive: he first writes absolutely everything down. "The work is driven by a certain cadence. The whole shaping of the poem becomes important later on—going back and cutting, and thinking about each line as an increment of the whole, and each word as an increment within the line." A new book, *Thieves of Paradise*, will come out this fall from Wesleyan.

Currently, Komunyakaa is hard at work on a long collection of poems concerning "the African diaspora." Entitled *Pleasure Dome*, these poems go "hand in hand with the excavation of black America" taking place today. Frustrated that very few people recognize famous black figures like Alexandre Dumas, Ira Aldridge, St. Benedict the Moor, Alessandro de Medici, Jean-Louis, Hatshepsut, Zenobia, Mary Seacole, Sosthene Mortenol, and Makeda, nor these men and women's important roles in history, Komunyakaa hopes the new poems will paint the missing colors in "the larger canvas" of history and race.

During his lifetime Komunyakaa concedes that a great deal of progress has been made in the context of race. He believes apartheid existed not only in South Africa, but also "right in this country, and is still here to an extent," but that there has been substantial change, especially in the South. Guardedly optimistic, he believes now is the time for America "to face up to what's happening and to move forward." Komunyakaa's poems will "continue to confront the fear" he sees in society, while simultaneously celebrating life. He writes because he needs to. Whether he's "having a good time, or trying to figure out more desperate questions that plague the psyche," he always finds himself scribbling notes down. He couldn't stop writing if he wanted to.

BOOKSHELF

FIRST, BODY *Stories by Melanie Rae Thon. Houghton Mifflin, $21.95 cloth. Reviewed by Christopher Tilghman.*

Melanie Rae Thon's fierce, unyielding, and brilliant new stories are now collected in *First, Body,* and the effect of reading all of them together after seeing many of them when originally published is simply to encounter genius.

These stories come from what Thon has called, elsewhere, the borderlands, the margins of our affluent culture. Thon's borderlands are populated primarily by young people, young women especially, whose bodies, minds, and spirits are being used up by themselves and by others for the briefest and often most heartbreakingly meager pleasures: a dance with a stranger; breaking into a house and eating pecan pie; a bowl of cherries. But never sex. These girls, and these women, give themselves up early and for every reason—money, fear, to please others—but never for love or even for their own pleasure. Human bodies, in these stories, are really never whole, flesh and soul: they are parts, pieces of lives that don't get to be lived.

There is not an ounce of fat in this book, no more than one can imagine on these undernourished skeletons. The stories all start on fire: "Two nurses with scissors could make a man naked in eleven seconds," is the celebrated opening line of the title story. "Dora's disappeared again," is the first sentence of the collection's masterwork, "Necessary Angels." They close with an equal lack of ceremony, as in "The Snow Thief": "I'm a grown woman, an orphan, I have these choices."

In between there is not much plot. Indeed, the sheer power of Thon's vision and the hold the characters have over her seem to be driving her far away from the conventional structures of her earlier stories and novels. The stories in *First, Body* are testimonies; the whole truth of the piece is in every line, which means that linear plot and character development are beside the point. Yet each one of them has a power that holds a reader transfixed.

This collection feels like a book of photographs, and one reads knowing that every new page will contain unforgettable—perhaps horrible—images.

What is finally most distinctive about this work is the author's willingness to become each one of her characters. Character, narrator, and author are the same person here. This fierce identification is manifestly felt in the prose, but it's made even more explicit by a voice that breaks in now and again. "I'm Dora," says the narrator in "Necessary Angels." "I know you're afraid of where I'm going when I tell you this. I'm afraid. But I can't stop. Forgetting is the first lie, a little death."

Melanie Rae Thon means every word here. Writing these stories cannot have been easy, and the process couldn't have been much fun. Young writers and graduate students ought to read this book and ask themselves whether they might have the courage to take their careers into a place like this.

There are plenty of writers out there working for profit on the ugly edges of society, and I suppose we have to read some of them. But Melanie Rae Thon is a very different case. The girls in *Girls in the Grass, Iona Moon,* and others went there first, and Thon followed them because she'd sworn to be honest to them. She hasn't lost her compassion out there in her borderlands; she has gone out there because of moral purpose. I have admired Thon's previous work, but *First, Body* leaves me completely in awe.

Christopher Tilghman is the author of In a Father's Place *and, most recently, the novel* Mason's Retreat. *He is completing a new collection of stories.*

THE BROKEN WORLD *Poems by Marcus Cafagña. Univ. of Illinois Press, $9.95 paper. Reviewed by Joyce Peseroff.*

The inhabitants of Marcus Cafagña's broken world beat against the bars of circumstance and fate as the poet fixes them with the empathy of attention. Whether in the kid shooting baskets who's "had it / with the Crisis Center" ("The Way He Breaks") or the girl on the freeway overpass whose face, pressed against the fence, is crosshatched with anger, Cafagña imagines both dignity and possibility: the boy leaps like "someone drowning, / pushing his weight / up off the bottom," and the girl throws not herself but a bandanna "red as a cardinal," "like a life to the horizon" ("Black Girl on the Overpass").

Cafagña's art attempts to make something whole, sane, and tender from the shattered lives he witnesses and cares for. To the aunt whose throat was knifed by her drug-addicted son, Cafagña offers the notion that "a scar is something / faithful, a way her skin / / will never give him up" ("Something Faithful"). The poet embraces those irreparably harmed by twentieth-century realities, including the runaway boy in the title poem whose "...parents beat him / or their priest wedged fingers / between his legs as if searching / / for the smallest bud of lilac." In several poems for his aunt Sarah, Cafagña writes movingly of a Holocaust survivor who "went mad on a train" and who envisions in her Brooklyn apartment "the superintendent's / SS armband, how at night / he floated through floors... /... filled / vacuum cleaner bags / with dirt" ("Dybbuks").

The poems rush headlong, preferring enjambed to end-stopped lines, as if trying to outrace the sad histories they narrate. The poet tactfully reserves for the book's last section the personal tragedy of his wife's suicide. Perhaps the most poignant example of Cafagña's eye for plain but eloquent detail occurs in "All the Bells": "When I drive past our old brick townhouse / I see them— red and yellow— / the tulips you planted last spring / risen from the ground after winter." Color, isolated visually as well as verbally in a world devoid of color ("old brick townhouse"), rises as the woman will not, while the poem's music lowers the reader from "house" to "ground." *The Broken World* serves to remind that "...danger, like beauty, distorts its shape / in rehearsal, meaning fades like starlight / splayed through curtains, and soon its signals / cannot be read" ("June Bug"). Cafagña doesn't muddle the past with false nostalgia or the future with false hope, but his first book interprets the signals of silenced lives and provides a measure of redemption.

Joyce Peseroff's most recent book of poems is A Dog in the Lifeboat *(Carnegie-Mellon).*

BITTER LAKE *A novel by Ann Harleman. Southern Methodist Univ. Press, $22.50 cloth, $12.95 paper. Reviewed by Fred Leebron.*

In her first novel, *Bitter Lake,* Ann Harleman, the 1993 winner of the John Simmons Short Fiction Award, deftly evokes the complex world of abandonment in a dysfunctional family. Here is a meditative work about family, motherhood, and an encumbered adolescence, in which characters seek to make the absent present and to rejuvenate their inert and desperate lives.

Gort and Judith are first cousins from the Midwest who married and moved to Bethlehem, Pennsylvania, where they parented two girls six years apart while Gort worked at Bethlehem Steel and disappeared at irregular intervals, always to return. Judith explains, "Gort and I had always, as he put it, lived against the grain (of America, he meant)—jobs that paid in freedom rather than in cash, a life not held hostage to *things*... The going away and coming back renewed—that was the way Gort was."

As the novel begins, Gort has been gone two weeks, and their fourteen-year-old daughter, Lil, is pressuring Judith to report him missing. The distinction between Lil and Judith's perspectives provides the narrative drive for the story. Harleman shifts smoothly between the two voices as mother and daughter struggle to find meaning in Gort's prolonged absence. When the days mount without explanation or discovery, Judith seeks to build a new life, gaining a job as a carpenter's assistant and entering into a romantic relationship that is antithetical to the one she had shared with Gort. But her problems with Lil intensify, her daughter becoming more and more a mystery to her: "I thought of how she'd been at three, at six, at nine. No one warns you about the losses. No one tells you you'll miss them, those earlier children. They disappear but are they still there, sealed one inside the next like those little Russian dolls?"

As always, Judith's perception is acute, for it is Lil's awareness of the past that keeps motivating Lil's own actions—into a relationship with *her* first cousin, and into a desperate search to find her father, an effort that leads her both forward and backward in time, to a turning moment at Bitter Lake that comprises the family's central tragedy. "For a moment," Judith says, when watching over her daughter at a hospital after a midnight accident, "I saw the little girl trapped inside, a child the old woman had swallowed, a child that I, reaching in deep and pulling it out through the slack mouth, might save."

Throughout *Bitter Lake* there is an obsession with understanding the emptiness caused not only by the departure of Gort, but also by essential questions of self. "Gort had been my cousin before he was my friend; my friend before he was my lover,"

Judith declares. "Gort had been my family, always. We didn't need to talk, the silence of families held us." Eventually, Judith recognizes an opposite aspect of this silence. "Suddenly I knew what it was Gort longed for. Had always longed for. Not our combined magic, that third we made between us; but the opposite. Order, distance, solitude—the other side of silence. A pearl in the brain."

Fred Leebron's first novel, Out West, *will be reissued in paperback by Harcourt Brace/Harvest in 1997. He is the co-editor of the forthcoming* Postmodern American Fiction: A Norton Anthology.

JIMMY & RITA *Poems by Kim Addonizio. BOA Editions, $12.50 paper. Reviewed by Diann Blakely Shoaf.*

Whitman's famous proclamation "Through me the many long dumb voices," depending on how it strikes the ear, echoes either with self-aggrandizement, a song that appropriates everything within shouting distance to swell its own puny notes, or with self-erasure, negative capability yawped with a barbarously American accent. The latter inflects the various voices of *Jimmy & Rita,* the second full-length collection by Kim Addonizio, whose *The Philosophers' Club* won the 1994 Great Lakes' New Writer Award. In this new volume, a verse novel, Addonizio acts as a postmodern aeolian harp, stirred to music by the stories of two eponymous lovers from our mostly unheard and invisible underclass. The most tragic aspect of the fifty-five poems lies in the fact that both Rita and Jimmy know themselves only by their failures, foremost among them the various failures of their love. Thus, it's a triumphant, terrible paradox that Addonizio gives voices and identities to her self-negated "characters" with such lavish clarity that they quickly become "real people," but merely to readers, never to themselves.

Rita and Jimmy, whose lives include heroin, theft, drug dealing, prostitution, and homelessness, have existed since childhood in a painful, noisy place created by the disharmonies of dream and injury. Although the couple's milieu becomes an extreme of the American nightmare, the space in which they love and suffer, as children and adults, is large enough to contain us all. In "Portrait," for example, we're told that Rita, the oldest of seven kids, "used to hide / from the noise in the house—/ sliding down in the bathtub, / warm water in her ears," and "if she hummed / her head filled up with music." Her father, a door-to-door portraitist employed by Golden West Photography, mainly photographs the family he later abandons: "Rita has pictures / of herself at every age to twelve / in front of a velvet backdrop, / holding the latest baby, / smiling to please him." Jimmy describes a fist-ready and boozy dad who, among other cruelties, feeds his son beer and laughs when he falls over furniture or vomits. Nonetheless, like Rita, like any normal child, Jimmy hungers for his father's approval: "Sometimes I'd sit up / at night in the garage and watch / how he drank it, tipping his head / way back, and I'd try to drink mine exactly the same, / but quietly, so he wouldn't notice and send me away." Rita believes she'll be loved if she is quiet and pretty; Jimmy's credo includes invisibility and strength, or at least being needed. After the couple is married and Jimmy loses his job, he wakes in the middle of the night and wants to hit Rita, "lying there curled / toward the window. / Just once, / hard, so she'd cry out / and he could comfort her."

In the hands of a lesser poet, the subject matter of *Jimmy & Rita* might have prompted what Jarrell called "a mooing awe for the common man." That obsequious and typically American awe, which sounds its moo when Whitman goes off-key, swells unchecked in the work of many contemporary poets, "compassion" now a loftier buzzword than any praiseful term for imagery, music, or even intelligence. While, obviously, technical brilliance fails to move us when unwedded to larger urgencies, an eleventh commandment should forbid exploiting subjects to display one's inherent or achieved sensitivity to suffering. The full achievement of *Jimmy & Rita* is greater than I have space to discuss, but Addonizio's cinematic use of shifting points of view and voice-overs is enormously effective; and her speedy, jazzily syncopated free verse in the third-person narratives and dramatic monologues, combined with her tersely astute prose poems, establishes her as a virtuoso of the craft just as surely as her characters prove her a fearless explorer of the most brutal, and often unsung, regions of the human heart.

Diann Blakely Shoaf's second book, Farewell, My Lovelies, *is forthcoming from Story Line Press. New work will appear in* Denver Quarterly, New England Review, The Paris Review, The Yale Review, *and elsewhere.*

*Books Recommended by
Our Advisory Editors*

Ann Beattie recommends *Reader's Block,* a novel by David Markson: "Finally: a fictional sequel to Eliot's 'The Wasteland.' Markson's novel advances by allusion and cumulative effect, like a big snowball going downhill (and it's impossible to read without realizing that the twentieth century has gone the same way). This is really a work of genius: real flotsam and jetsam, recycled as philosophy. It's hypnotic and unique; of course, that would guarantee that the mainstream press wouldn't give a damn." (Dalkey Archive)

Robert Boswell recommends *Silk,* stories by Grace Dane Mazur: "Mazur is a former microbiologist, and the stories in her first collection offer a means of apprehending the world that is both intellectually fascinating and sensually wired. It is either a book of the mind about pleasures of the flesh, or a book of the flesh about the currents of the mind. Mazur gives not even a nod to trendy explanations for the complex workings of the heart, choosing instead to do what good literature has always done: cast new light on old mysteries. This is a strange and terrific book." (Lumen)

Rosellen Brown recommends *Under the Tuscan Sun: At Home in Italy,* a memoir by Frances Mayes: "Frances Mayes's beautifully written account of her love affair with a house she and her husband renovated in Tuscany, and with a place that retains ancient standards for all things sensual, contains an essay that appeared in my personal essay issue, Fall 1994." (Chronicle)

Madeline DeFrees recommends *Intricate Moves,* poems and an essay by Joan Swift: "One of the Northwest's best poets collects her poems dealing with rape—both those originally included in *The Dark Path of Our Names* (Dragon Gate) and later poems. Swift is the winner of three NEA grants, the most recent being the only one awarded in Washington state. Her poems have also won an Ingram Merrill grant and have appeared in *DoubleTake, The New Yorker,* and *Poetry.*" (Chicory Blue)

DeWitt Henry recommends *Richard Yates,* criticism by David Castronovo and Steven Goldleaf: "As part of Twayne's United States Authors Series, this book is a provocative, helpful, and well-informed reading of Yates's work as a canon, related to his biography, the work of his contemporaries, and to the intellectual character of our times and culture. Provides a solid basis for further study and appreciation." (Twayne)

Maxine Kumin recommends *The Black Notebooks,* a memoir by Toi Derricotte: "Searing. Read it." (Norton)

Don Lee recommends *Burning Down the House: Essays on Fiction,* nonfiction by Charles Baxter: "In nine brilliant essays, Baxter displays his characteristic wit and intelligence as he muses about the influences of culture and politics on the art of storytelling." (Graywolf)

Philip Levine recommends *Things that Happen Once,* poems by Rodney Jones: "Rodney Jones is a new and long overdue discovery of mine. With wit, charm, and great resourcefulness, he writes wonderfully uncluttered poems that pay tribute to a rich cast of characters, from Aunt Madge to Melody, 'the teenage welfare mother down the hall.' His poems of a Southern boyhood and coming of age are as good as those of Dave Smith's, though in no way indebted to them. 'The End of Communism' is the impossible American political poem, written without rancor, sentimentality, or forgiveness. In this collection Jones does a great many different things and does them all with great artistry and modesty." (Houghton Mifflin)

Thomas Lux recommends *Squandering,* poems by George Mills: "Gorgeous, utterly original poems by a poet now in his mid-seventies. Exceptionally beautiful production—a limited letterpress edition. His first book was *The House Sails Out of Sight of Home,* winner of the 1991 Morse Poetry Prize, from Northeastern University Press." (Indian Hill)

James Alan McPherson recommends *All the Money in the World,* a novel by Robert Anthony Siegel: "A heartfelt first novel by a gifted former student." (Random)

Gary Soto recommends *In a Few Words/En pocas palabras,* poems and translations by José Antonio Burciaga: "Burciaga has gathered *dichos*—pithy sayings and proverbs—that reveal the folk wisdom of rural peasants. These are deft translations, as wise as the originals, as in *'Si cada pendejo trajera palo, faltaría leña':* 'If every fool carried a stick, firewood would be scarce. We nod our heads, and agree.'" (Mercury)

Maura Stanton recommends *My Shining Archipelago,* poems by Taluikki Ansel: "Ansel's poems are surprising and imaginative, filled with fresh insight into the natural world. Winner of the 1996 Yale Series of Younger Poets competition." (Yale)

EDITORS' CORNER

*New Books by
Our Advisory Editors*

Anne Bernays and **Justin Kaplan,** *The Language of Names: What We're Called*

and Why It Matters, nonfiction: Bernays and Kaplan present a fascinating and very readable account of names and naming in contemporary society, touching on class structure, ethnic and religious practices, manners, and everyday life. (Simon & Schuster)

Robert Boswell, *American Owned Love,* a novel: In his fourth novel, Boswell examines the unique border culture along the Rio Grande, unforgettably weaving together disparate people—Anglos, Mexicans, lovers, children—as they wade through this particular world's infinite possibilities and strangeness. (Knopf)

Maxine Kumin, *Selected Poems 1960–1990,* poems: A rich and varied selection of poems from nine previous collections, spanning three decades of work. Kumin's voice is full of strength and grace as she meditates on her New Hampshire farm, her family, and the natural world. (Norton)

Philip Levine, *Unselected Poems,* poems: This provocative, quirky volume collects the best of Levine's work—some of his favorites—that he was unable to include in his *New Selected Poems,* which is now out of print, and in his previous three books. (Greenhouse Review)

Thomas Lux, *New and Selected Poems,* poems: The winner of the Kingsley Tufts Award for *Split Horizon,* Lux gathers poems from the last twenty years that demonstrate his deft humor and precise music, fastening on the rueful poignancies of our lives. (Houghton Mifflin)

Richard Tillinghast, *Today in the Café Trieste,* poems: Tillinghast's first book to be published in Ireland contains new poems written, with typical mastery, since *The Stonecutter's Hand* (Godine, 1995), as well as a retrospective of his earlier work. (Salmon)

POSTSCRIPTS

CONTRIBUTOR SPOTLIGHT Growing up in Fall River, Massachusetts, David Rivard had been forced to copy patriotic verse on the blackboard during detention, and until he was well into college, he continued to regard poetry as a punitive activity. Certainly he never imagined that he himself would become a poet—one whose books have racked up some of the most prestigious awards in the field. Rivard's first collection of poems, *Torque,* won the Agnes Lynch Starrett Poetry Prize and was published by the Pitt Poetry Series in 1988. His second book, *Wise Poison,* published last year by Graywolf Press, won the James Laughlin Award from the Academy of American Poets. The Academy, besides giving Rivard a cash prize of $5,000, bought over six thousand hardcover copies of the book to distribute to its members, which made *Wise Poison,* in relative terms, a bestseller.

How did a blue-collar kid from a New England mill town become such a respected poet? Rivard is perplexed about that himself at times. Born in 1953, he was raised among civil servants and dressmakers. His great-grandfather was the first Portuguese policeman in Fall River. His grandfather was also a cop, and his father was a fireman. His French-Canadian grandmother worked as a seamstress, as did most of the women in the neighborhood. The entire family lived in a triple-decker—grandparents on the third floor, great-uncle and great-aunt on the first, with Rivard and his parents and his brother and two sisters sandwiched in between.

As the oldest, Rivard was expected to go to college—the first in the family to attend—and then become a professional of some sort, a lawyer, an engineer, a doctor, any occupation that would represent a move up in class. For a while, Rivard cooperated. He had liked building models as a child and thought of becoming an architect. But in high school, he discovered an unfortunate fact. He stunk at math. He settled on anthropology, and at nearby Southeastern Massachusetts University, he showed enough promise to earn a full scholarship to graduate school at Princeton.

Along the way, though, a friend introduced Rivard to a different kind of poetry—not the bland, stultifying compositions he remembered from Catholic boys' school, but something new, rebellious. He read books by the Beats, Gary Snyder, Wallace Stevens, and W. S. Merwin, and when he went to hear the latter at a reading, he became a true believer. "I fell in love with language," he says, "this idea of making a performance with just words." He began taking some poetry workshops, notably with Theodore Weiss at Princeton, and he realized imme-diately that he enjoyed writing. "For the same reason I liked making models as a kid, I liked making something out of nothing, something that had a shape, with a kind of architecture of language that informed and created that shape." This newfound distrac-tion did not go unnoticed by his faculty advisor at Princeton, who finally sat Rivard

Mark Morelli

down for a talk. He told him he had to choose between anthropol-ogy and poetry. "If you can't," the advisor said, referring to Rivard's full scholarship, "someone else wants your money."

"It was a clarifying moment," Rivard recalls. "It made me very conscious about whether I wanted to be a writer or not, and that I would be taking a risk and sacrificing a lot in order to do that, so I should take it seriously." He dropped out of Princeton, stunning his parents and worrying them to no end. "My dad's response was classic. He said, 'Well, you could take the fire exam. You could set up a table there in the firehouse and write your poetry. No one's going to bother you.'"

Rivard lived and wrote in Boston for a couple of years, support-ing himself with editorial work for bilingual educational projects, then enrolled in the M.F.A. program at the University of Arizona in 1979. He studied with Jon Anderson, Steve Orlen, and Tess Gallagher, and among his classmates were Li-Young Lee, Tony Hoagland, David Wojahn, Ai, and Michael Collier. At first, Rivard wrote surreal, abstract poems, but his early efforts, he is the first to admit, were largely confused and unsuccessful. It wasn't until he discovered Philip Levine's work that he found a niche and began addressing life in Fall River. "I started thinking, Oh, this is a landscape that's familiar to me, this kind of working-class, industrial mill town, and here's a way to approach it. My sensibilities turned out to be different than Levine's, but he and Richard Hugo and James Wright gave me a way to write about the world I came from."

A decade later, those poems about Fall River would comprise most of *Torque*, as well as some of *Wise Poison*. The new book, however, ranges farther afield, both geographically and stylistically, incorporating a more complex, ironic narrative that is funny, sly, at times angry, and occasionally self-recriminative. A poem like "Self-Portrait," for example, presents a series of brilliant associations, from a dead hornet on a windowsill, to a Hungarian engineer who bootlegs R&B records on old x-ray sheets, "so a diamond-tipped stylus could glide / the bluesy decrescendos, the riffs / and splintered eighth notes, of jawbone & hip socket," to wrecking a friend's VW in an attempted insurance scam, to an imagined kinship with another hornet, the one that must have escaped, "wings folded back, lost, but canny enough / not to give the feeling a name."

These days, Rivard has started to edge away from narrative toward a lyric poetry that is less about the consequence of events on character and more about "how life simply *is*, that's all, just *is*, the play of moods over the long day. Jon Anderson used to tell his students that a poem is a kind of self-confrontation, and so you say the hardest thing. I don't believe that as much anymore, because it tends to produce a psychological drama of the self, a judgmental, or critical, or moralistic sensibility, that I'm frankly tired of."

His personal life has influenced some of this shift. Now living in Cambridge, Massachusetts, Rivard teaches at Tufts University and in Vermont College's low-residency M.F.A. program, and is *Harvard Review*'s poetry editor. He and his wife, book-jacket designer Michaela Sullivan, have a three-year-old daughter, Simone, and the poems in his half-completed third manuscript, *Bewitched Playground*, have been affected by the demands of his busy schedule: "The new poems are about the imaginative space that I inhabit on a day-to-day basis. Up to this point, a lot of my poems have been structured as meditative narratives, and often reflected on past events from a present perspective. Now, they're very much located in the present. Having a kid has forced me to live in ways that seem much more improvised and unexpected. Since Simone was born, I don't know where I am half the time—but it's a pleasurable confusion. Life feels a lot fresher, and I want that freshness, the surprise of it, in the poems."

BEST AMERICAN POETRY Five poems from two issues of *Plough-shares* have been selected for *The Best American Poetry 1997,* which will be published by Scribner this fall. Guest-edited by James Tate, with David Lehman as the series editor, this year's prize anthology will include Nin Andrews's "That Cold Summer," Daniel Halpern's "Her Body," and Gray Jacobik's "Dust Storm," all from the Winter 1995–96 issue, edited by Tim O'Brien and Mark Strand; and Thomas Sayers Ellis's "Atomic Bride" and Khaled Mattawa's "Heartsong," both from the Spring 1996 issue, edited by Marilyn Hacker.

SUBSCRIBERS Please feel free to contact us via e-mail with address changes (the post office usually will not forward journals) or any problems with your subscription. Our e-mail address is: pshares@emerson.edu. Also, please note that on occasion we exchange mailing lists with other literary magazines and organizations. If you would like your name excluded from these exchanges, simply send us an e-mail message or a letter stating so.

CONTRIBUTORS' NOTES

Spring 1997

TONY ARDIZZONE's most recent book is *Taking It Home: Stories from the Neighborhood* (Illinois, 1996). "The Fisherman's Son" is from his just-completed novel, *In the Garden of Papa Santuzzu*. He teaches ethnic literature and creative writing at Indiana University, where he also directs the creative writing program.

WILLIAM BAER, a recent grant recipient from the NEA, has had his work published in *Poetry, The Hudson Review, The New Criterion,* and *The Southern Review.* He is also the editor of *The Formalist,* a journal of poetry, and *Conversations with Derek Walcott,* a collection of the Nobelist's interviews.

JAMES BERTOLINO's eighth volume of poems, *Snail River,* was published in 1995 in the *Quarterly Review of Literature* poetry series. Other books include *First Credo, New & Selected Poems,* and *Precinct Kali & The Gertrude Spicer Story.* He received his M.F.A. from Cornell, teaches at Western Washington University, and lives on Guemes Island, Washington.

BRUCE BOND's poems have recently appeared in *The Yale Review, The Georgia Review, The Threepenny Review, Poetry,* and other journals, and his third full-length poetry collection, *Radiography,* is forthcoming from BOA Editions. Currently he is Director of Creative Writing at the University of North Texas and Poetry Editor for the *American Literary Review.*

LAURE-ANNE BOSSELAAR's poetry collection, *The Hour Between Dog and Wolf,* will be published by BOA Editions in May 1997. With her husband, Kurt Brown, she co-edited *Night Out: Poems about Hotels, Motels, Restaurants & Bars* (Milkweed, 1997). She teaches a poetry workshop at Emerson College and lives in Cambridge, Massachusetts.

KEVIN BOWEN is Director of the William Joiner Center for the Study of War and Social Consequences at the University of Massachusetts, Boston. His recent works include *Playing Basketball with the Viet Cong* (Curbstone, 1994) and, with Bruce Weigl, *Writing Between the Lines: An Anthology on War and Its Social Consequences* (Massachusetts, 1997).

LATON CARTER is from Eugene, Oregon. He studied music at the University of North Texas, received a B.A. in English from the University of Oregon, and is currently an M.F.A. candidate in poetry at the University of California, Irvine.

RICHARD CECIL has published two collections of poems, *Einstein's Brain* and *Alcatraz.* He teaches in the English department and the honors division of Indiana University.

BRUCE COHEN is Director of the Counseling Program for Intercollegiate Athletes at the University of Connecticut. His poems have appeared in various literary magazines, most recently *Cimarron Review, Indiana Review, The Ohio Review,* and *Mid-American Review.* This is his second appearance in *Ploughshares.*

MARTHA COLLINS's most recent book of poems is *A History of Small Life on a Windy Planet,* which won the Alice Fay Di Castagnola Award. She teaches at the University of Massachusetts, Boston, where she founded and co-directs the creative writing program.

GREG DELANTY's most recent book of poems is *American Wake* (Dufour, 1995). He also edited *Jumping Off Shadows: Selected Contemporary Irish Poets* (Cork University, 1995). In 1996 he received the Wolfer O'Neill Literature Award and the Austin Clarke Centenary Poetry Award. He teaches at Saint Michael's College in Vermont.

TOI DERRICOTTE has two books forthcoming in 1997: *Tender,* a book of poetry from the University of Pittsburgh Press, and *The Black Notebooks,* a literary memoir to be published by W.W. Norton.

MARK DOTY's new collection of poems, *Sweet Machine,* will be published by HarperCollins in the spring of 1998. He teaches at the University of Utah and divides his time between Salt Lake City and Provincetown, Massachusetts.

GIL JOSÉ DURÁN is a student at DePauw University in Greencastle, Indiana. A Knight-Ridder journalism scholar, he has reported for *The Miami Herald* and *The Herald-Leader* in Lexington, Kentucky.

MARTÍN ESPADA is the author of five poetry collections, most recently *City of Coughing and Dead Radiators* and *Imagine the Angels of Bread,* both from W.W. Norton. His awards include two NEA fellowships, the PEN/Revson fellowship, a Massachusetts Cultural Council artist grant, and the Paterson Poetry Prize. He teaches in the English department at the University of Massachusetts, Amherst.

GEORGE EVANS is the author of four books of poetry published in the United States and England, the most recent of which is *Sudden Dreams* (Coffee House). His work has been represented in a number of recent anthologies, including *Against Forgetting, Postmodern American Poetry,* and *The Other Side of Heaven.* Among other awards, he has received a Lannan Foundation fellowship and two NEA fellowships. He lives in San Francisco.

SASCHA FEINSTEIN is the author of *Jazz Poetry: From the 1920s to the Present* and the co-editor, with Yusef Komunyakaa, of *The Jazz Poetry Anthology* and *The Second Set.* He teaches at Lycoming College and edits *Brilliant Corners: A Journal of Jazz & Literature.*

CAROLYN FERRELL's first story collection, *Don't Erase Me,* will be published by Houghton Mifflin this spring. Her stories have appeared in journals such as *Callaloo, Story,* and *The Literary Review.* Her story "Proper Library," which first appeared in *Ploughshares,* was subsequently anthologized in *The Best American Short Stories 1994,* edited by Tobias Wolff, and *Children of the Night: The Best Short Stories by Black Writers: 1967 to the Present,* edited by Gloria Naylor. She currently teaches at Sarah Lawrence College.

CECILE GODING is from Florence, South Carolina, where she directed adult literacy projects. She is the author of a chapbook of poems, *The Women Who Drink at the Sea* (State Street), and is a graduate student in nonfiction and poetry at the University of Iowa.

JENNIFER GROTZ's poems have appeared or are forthcoming in *The Black Warrior Review, Negative Capability, Hayden's Ferry Review,* and *Puerto del Sol.* She received her M.F.A. from Indiana University in 1996 and now lives in Portland, Oregon.

ALEXANDER GUREVICH, born in 1959 in Leningrad, is a mathematician by education. He has published two books in his own translation, and his poems have appeared in *The Human Foundation* and *The Star.* Since 1993, he has worked as an interpreter for American oil explorers. "Komi" and other poems by Gurevich will appear in an upcoming anthology of Petersburg poets.

MARILYN HACKER is the author of eight books, most recently *Winter Numbers,* from W.W. Norton, which received the 1995 Lenore Marshall Award and a Lambda Literary Award, and *Selected Poems,* also from Norton, which won the 1996 Poets' Prize. *Edge,* her translations of work by the French poet Claire Malroux, was published in 1996 by Wake Forest University Press.

BOB HICOK is an automotive die designer. His second book, *The Legend of Light,* won the 1995 Felix Pollak Prize from the University of Wisconsin. New poems are due out in *The Best American Poetry 1997, Boulevard, DoubleTake,* and *The Iowa Review.* His third book, *Kinship,* will come out with BOA Editions in 1998.

COLETTE INEZ, author of seven books of poetry, has received fellowships from the Guggenheim and Rockefeller foundations, the New York Foundation for the Arts, and the NEA. Widely published, she teaches poetry workshops at Columbia University. She recently completed a new collection of poems and a prose memoir. This summer she will be teaching at Antioch College's writers' conference.

HATIF JANABI was born in Iraq in 1953. Since 1976 he has lived as an exile in Poland, where he has published five bilingual volumes of poetry. The winner of numerous poetry prizes in Poland, he earned a Ph.D. in drama from Warsaw University, where he now teaches Arabic literature and world drama. His poems, essays, and translations have appeared in many Arabic literary magazines.

WILLIAM H. JOHNSON was born in 1901 in Florence, South Carolina, studied at the National Academy of Design in New York City, and lived in Paris, Harlem, Denmark, and South Carolina. Although he received considerable recognition as an artist early in his career, he died in relative obscurity in a New York state mental institution in 1970. The painting on the cover, "Three Great Freedom Fighters," depicting John Brown, Harriet Tubman, and Frederick Douglass, measures 35 ½″ x 27 ⅜″ and was composed with oil on fiberboard. It is reproduced courtesy of Hampton University Museum in Hampton, Virginia.

ALICE JONES won the Beatrice Hawley Award from Alice James Books for *The Knot* in 1992. A 1994 NEA fellow, she has published her poems in *Pequod, Zyzzyva, Poetry,* and *The Best American Poetry 1994.* A chapbook, *Anatomy,* is forthcoming.

ALLISON JOSEPH is the author of three collections of poetry: *What Keeps Us Here* (Ampersand, 1992), which won the John C. Zacharis First Book Award from Emerson College and *Ploughshares, Soul Train* (Carnegie-Mellon, 1997), and *In Every Seam* (Pittsburgh, 1997). She currently lives in Carbondale, Illinois, and teaches at Southern Illinois University.

JESSE LEE KERCHEVAL is the author of two books of fiction, *The Dogeater* and *The Museum of Happiness.* A memoir, *Space,* about growing up near Cape Kennedy during the moon race, is forthcoming from Algonquin Books.

PRISCILLA LEE works as a technical writer for a network computing company. Her poems have appeared in *The Kenyon Review, Mid-American Review, Zyzzyva, Bakunin, Phoebe,* and *The Cream City Review.* Her work is forthcoming in *Storming Heaven's Gate: An Anthology of Women's Spiritual Writing* (Penguin/New American), *Café Review, Gargoyle,* and *Making Waves II: An Anthology of Asian American Women Writers* (Beacon).

LARRY LEVIS published five collections of poems during his life, the most recent of which was *The Widening Spell of the Leaves* (Pittsburgh, 1991). A new book, *Elegy,* will be published by the University of Pittsburgh Press this fall. At the time of his death in May 1996, he was Professor of English at Virginia Commonwealth University in Richmond. His awards included the U.S. Award of the International Poetry Forum, a Lamont Prize, and a selection by the National Poetry Series.

DEMETRIA MARTINEZ of Tucson, Arizona, is the author of *Mother Tongue* (Ballantine), which won the 1994 Western States Book Award for Fiction. She is also the author of *Breathing Between the Lines* (Arizona), a collection of poetry. A columnist for the independent *National Catholic Reporter,* she is involved with immigrants' rights issues along the U.S.–Mexico border.

KHALED MATTAWA is the author of *Ismailia Eclipse* (Sheep Meadow, 1995) and the translator of two books of contemporary Arabic poetry, Hatif Janabi's *Questions and Their Retinue* (Arkansas) and Fadhil Al-Azzawi's *In Every Well a Joseph Is Weeping* (*Quarterly Review of Literature*). His poems have appeared in *Poetry, The Kenyon Review, The Pushcart Prize,* and elsewhere. A poem of his in *Ploughshares* last year will be included in *The Best American Poetry 1997.*

JOHN MCCLUSKEY, JR., teaches fiction writing and contemporary African American literature at Indiana University. He is the author of two novels: *Look What They Done to My Song* (1974) and *Mr. America's Last Season Blues* (1983). With Charles Johnson, he co-edited *Black Men Speaking,* a reader on African American men that will appear this spring.

CAMPBELL MCGRATH's latest book of poems is *Spring Comes to Chicago* (Ecco), which received the 1996 Kingsley Tufts Poetry Award. He teaches at Florida International University and lives in Miami Beach with his family.

PHIL METRES's translations and poems have appeared in *Artful Dodge, Glas, Modern Poetry in Translation, New Laurel Review, Poetry New York, Spoon River Poetry Review,* and *Willow Springs.* A graduate student in English at Indiana University, he is finishing *Celebration: Selected Poems by Sergey Gandlevsky.*

CARL PHILLIPS's most recent book of poems, *Cortège,* was a finalist for the 1995 National Book Critics Circle Award. A new book, *From the Devotions,* is forthcoming this fall. He is Associate Professor of English and of African and Afro-American Studies at Washington University, St. Louis, where he also directs the creative writing program.

MARILENE PHIPPS was born and raised in Haiti. She was a 1995 Guggenheim fellow, the 1993 Grolier Poetry Prize winner, and a 1992–93 fellow at the Bunting Institute of Radcliffe and Harvard. She studied anthropology at the University of California, Berkeley, and is an M.F.A. graduate of Pennsylvania University.

ROHAN B. PRESTON was the recipient of a 1996 Illinois Arts Council artist fellowship and won the 1997 Henry Blakely, Jr., Poetry Prize, which was awarded by Gwendolyn Brooks in honor of her late husband's memory. He is the author of *Dreams in Soy Sauce* (Tia Chucha, 1992) and the co-editor of *Soulfires: Young Black Men on Love and Violence* (Penguin, 1996). A member of the Chicago-based Blue Ellipsis Collective, he has published his work in *The Atlanta Review, Crab Orchard Review, Eyeball,* and *Hammers.*

LEROY V. QUINTANA is a native New Mexican. A Vietnam veteran (Airborne), he holds master's degrees in English and counseling, and is a licensed marriage, family, and child counselor. A former NEA fellow, he is the winner of two American Book Awards and the editor, with Victor Hernandez Cruz and Virgil Suarez, of *Paper Dance: 55 Latino Poets* (Persea).

JAN RICHMAN's first book, *Because the Brain Can Be Talked into Anything,* won the 1994 Walt Whitman Award from the Academy of American Poets, judged by Robert Pinsky, and was published last spring by Louisiana State University Press. A former NEA fellow, she has published her poetry in many magazines, including *The Nation, Ploughshares, The Bloomsbury Review,* and *Grand Street.*

JENNIFER RICHTER, a former Wallace Stegner fellow at Stanford University, is currently teaching poetry in Stanford's creative writing program. Her work has been published or is forthcoming in *The Louisville Review, The Formalist, Callaloo, Yellow Silk, Alaska Quarterly Review, Third Coast,* and other journals.

DAVID RIVARD's new book, *Wise Poison* (Graywolf), won the 1996 James Laughlin Award from the Academy of American Poets. He has twice received fellowships from the NEA, and his poems and essays have appeared in *Poetry, Ploughshares, The North American Review, New England Review,* and elsewhere. Currently the poetry editor of *Harvard Review,* he teaches at Tufts University and in Vermont College's M.F.A. program. See page 216 for a "Contributor Spotlight" profile on Rivard.

LLOYD SCHWARTZ is Frederick S. Troy Professor of English at the University of Massachusetts, Boston, and a regular commentator on NPR's *Fresh Air*. For his articles on classical music in *The Boston Phoenix*, he received the 1994 Pulitzer Prize for criticism. His most recent book of poems is *Goodnight, Gracie.*

J. D. SCRIMGEOUR is an assistant professor of English at Salem State College. His poems have appeared in several publications, including *Poetry, Colorado Review*, and *Tar River Poetry*. "On, Wisconsin" is from a recently completed manuscript, *Background Checks.*

ANGELA SHANNON's poems have appeared in *TriQuarterly, Willow Review, Crab Orchard Review*, and *Black Text and Black Textuality: Deconstructing Blackness*, among other publications. A member of the Chicago-based Blue Ellipsis Collective, she is completing her first collection of poems, *Rootwoman.*

REGINALD SHEPHERD's second book, *Angel, Interrupted*, was published last fall by the University of Pittsburgh Press, which also published his first collection, *Some Are Drowning*, as winner of the 1993 AWP Award. A recipient of a 1995 NEA fellowship and other awards, he lives in Chicago. "Motive" is from a recently completed third manuscript entitled *Wrong.*

MAURA STANTON's stories have recently appeared or are forthcoming in *TriQuarterly, Crab Orchard Review*, and *The Cream City Review*. Her book of poetry, *Life Among the Trolls*, is forthcoming from Carnegie-Mellon University Press.

GERALD STERN's new book of selected poems will be published later this year by W.W. Norton. His most recent book is *Odd Mercy*, also from Norton. He recently retired from the Iowa Writers' Workshop and now lives in Pennsylvania.

NYUGEN QUANG THIEU has published four books of poems in Vietnam, as well as novels and short stories. In 1993, he won the Vietnam Writers' Association National Award for poetry. He lives in Hanoi, where he is the editor-in-chief of *Van Nghe Tre. The Women Carry River Water*, a bilingual edition of his poems co-translated with Martha Collins, will be published by the University of Massachusetts Press in May 1997.

MELANIE RAE THON's most recent book is the collection of stories *First, Body* (reviewed on page 208). She is also the author of two novels, *Meteors in August* and *Iona Moon*, and the collection *Girls in the Grass*. Originally from Montana, she now teaches at The Ohio State University.

RICHARD TILLINGHAST's sixth book of poetry, *Today in the Café Trieste*, a new and selected, has just been published in Ireland by Salmon. He has had two books recently published in this country: *The Stonecutter's Hand* (Godine) and *Robert Lowell's Life and Work: Damaged Grandeur* (Michigan).

BARBARA TRAN is currently at work editing *Watermark*, an anthology of Vietnamese American poetry and fiction, to be published by the Asian American

Writers' Workshop at the end of this year. Her own poems may be found in the anthologies *On a Bed of Rice* and *Premonitions.*

JON TRIBBLE has published poems in *Crazyhorse, Ploughshares, Poetry,* and *Sycamore Review.* He has work forthcoming in *Quarterly West.*

REETIKA VAZIRANI is the author of *White Elephants* (Beacon, 1996), which won the Barnard New Women Poets' Prize. Poems from a new manuscript have appeared recently in *Columbia, Shenandoah,* and *The Partisan Review.* She teaches poetry writing at the University of Virginia.

CHARLES H. WEBB worked as a rock singer and a psychotherapist before landing at California State University, Long Beach. He edited *Stand Up Poetry: The Anthology* and *The Poetry of Los Angeles.* A selection of his poems, introduced by Philip Levine, appears in *The Writing Path* (Iowa). His book *Reading the Water* recently won the 1997 Morse Poetry Prize and will be published by Northeastern University Press.

DAVID WOJAHN's fifth collection of poetry, *The Falling Hour,* will appear from the University of Pittsburgh Press in June. He teaches at Indiana University and in Vermont College's M.F.A. program.

LISA YANOVER is currently living in Houston, Texas, working on a Ph.D. in creative writing and literature and teaching college English. She received her M.A. from the University of California, Davis, and her B.A. from Oberlin College. She also lived for two years in Israel, where she studied Hebrew and Yiddish at the Hebrew University of Jerusalem. She has had poems in *Prairie Schooner* and *Amelia.*

DAISY ZAMORA, the author of three widely acclaimed books of poetry in Spanish, lives in Managua, Nicaragua. Two collections of her work have been published in translation in the United States: *Clean Slate* (Curbstone) and *Riverbed of Memory* (City Lights). She was featured in the recent Bill Moyers PBS series *The Language of Life* and is editor of *Pensamiento Proprio,* a journal dedicated to the investigation and study of economic and sociological conditions in Central America and the Caribbean.

SUBMISSION POLICIES *Ploughshares* is published three times a year: usually mixed issues of poetry and fiction in the Spring and Winter and a fiction issue in the Fall, with each guest-edited by a different writer. We welcome unsolicited manuscripts from August 1 to March 31 (postmark dates). All submissions sent from April to July are returned unread. In the past, guest editors often announced specific themes for issues, but we have revised our editorial policies and no longer restrict submissions to thematic topics. Submit your work at any time during our reading period; if a manuscript is not timely for one issue, it will be considered for another. Send one prose piece and/or one to three poems at a time (mail genres separately). Poems should be individually typed either single- or double-spaced on one side of the page. Prose should be typed double-spaced on one side and be no longer than twenty-five pages. Although we look primarily for short stories, we occasionally publish personal essays/memoirs. Novel excerpts are acceptable if self-contained. Unsolicited book reviews and criticism are not considered. Please do not send multiple submissions of the same genre, and do not send another manuscript until you hear about the first. Additional submissions will be returned unread. Mail your manuscript in a page-sized manila envelope, your full name and address written on the outside, to the "Fiction Editor," "Poetry Editor," or "Nonfiction Editor." (Unsolicited work sent directly to a guest editor's home or office will be discarded.) All manuscripts and correspondence regarding submissions should be accompanied by a self-addressed, stamped envelope (S.A.S.E.) for a response. Expect three to five months for a decision. Do not query us until five months have passed, and if you do, please write to us, including an S.A.S.E. and indicating the postmark date of submission, instead of calling. Simultaneous submissions are amenable as long as they are indicated as such and we are notified immediately upon acceptance elsewhere. We cannot accommodate revisions, changes of return address, or forgotten S.A.S.E.'s after the fact. We do not reprint previously published work. Translations are welcome if permission has been granted. We cannot be responsible for delay, loss, or damage. Payment is upon publication: $25/printed page, $50 minimum per title, $250 maximum per author, with two copies of the issue and a one-year subscription.

THE NAME *Ploughshares* 1. The sharp edge of a plough that cuts a furrow in the earth. 2 a. A variation of the name of the pub, the Plough and Stars, in Cambridge, Massachusetts, where a journal was founded. 2 b. The pub's name was inspired by the Sean O'Casey play about the Easter Rising of the Irish "citizen army." The army's flag contained a plough, representing the things of the earth, hence practicality; and stars, the ideals by which the plough is steered. 3. A shared, collaborative, community effort that has endured for twenty-six years. 4. A literary journal that has been energized by a desire for harmony, peace, and reform. Once, that spirit motivated civil rights marches, war protests, and student activism. Today, it still inspirits a desire for beating swords into ploughshares, but through the power and the beauty of the written word.

Ploughshares
Patrons

This publication would not be possible without the support of
our readers and the generosity of the following individuals
and organizations. As a nonprofit enterprise,
we welcome donations of any amount.

COUNCIL
Denise and Mel Cohen
Eugenia Gladstone Vogel

PATRONS
Anonymous
John K. Dineen
Scott and Annette Turow
Marillyn Zacharis

ORGANIZATIONS
Emerson College
Lila Wallace–Reader's Digest Fund
Council of Literary Magazines and Presses
Lannan Foundation
Massachusetts Cultural Council

COUNCIL: $3,000 for two lifetime subscriptions, acknowledgement
in the journal for three years, and votes on the Cohen and Zacharis
Awards. PATRON: $1,000 for a lifetime subscription and acknow-
ledgement in the journal for two years. FRIEND: $500 for a life-
time subscription and acknowledgement in the journal
for one year. All donations are tax-deductible.
Please make your check payable to *Ploughshares,*
Emerson College, 100 Beacon St., Boston, MA 02116.

Beyond the Bedroom Wall

LARRY WOIWODE

"Nothing more beautiful and moving has been written in years." *New York Times Book Review*

Like a series of photographs from a family album, Woiwode brings into loving focus charged moments in the lives of the Neumiller family over the course of four generations.

Paperback, $16.00 (1-55597-258-6) *Available June 1st*

Idle Curiosity

MARTHA BERGLAND

Between daughter Janet's fling with the new optometrist, and the surprise reappearance of long-lost and now pregnant daughter Vickie, retired farmer Ed Check discovers that age, distance, and time are unable to limit the desire of a father to keep his children safe.

Hardcover, $22.95 (1-55597-257-8) *Available May 1st*

Red Signature

MARY LEADER

Chosen by Deborah Digges as a winner for publication in the National Poetry Series
Leader finds glimmers of humanity in the most ordinary of places: recipe cards, a self-starved man's last will, a school-teacher's ditty. *Red Signature* commemorates history's forgotten figures: women, the poor, and the common, whose grace lives on in these small testaments.

Paperback, $12.95 (1-55597-255-1)

The Risk of His Music

PETER WELTNER

"Weltner portrays vividly his characters: gay vets of Vietnam, Southern hayseeds sprouted in all the wrong hometown settings, and perhaps most interestingly, male lovers who've lived and aged together long enough to witness the general decline of things in the middle America where they've chosen to live, and who must then finally, as do any 'married couple,' see each other through to burial at the bitter end." *Edmund White*

Paperback, $12.95 (1-55597-253-5)

2402 University Avenue, Suite 203 · St. Paul, MN 55114
(612) 641-0077 / Fax: (612) 641-0036 · Visit our website: www.graywolfpress.org

BENNINGTON
WRITING
SEMINARS

MFA in Writing and Literature
Two-Year Low-Residency Program

A. BLAKE GARDNER

FICTION
NONFICTION
POETRY

For more information contact:
Writing Seminars
Box PL
Bennington College
Bennington, VT 05201
802-442-5401, ext. 160
Fax 802-442-6164

A Selection of the
Barnes & Noble
Series
"DISCOVER
Great New
Writers"

CHEATERS
and Other Stories
by
DEAN ALBARELLI

"COMPELLING AND ORIGINAL TALES."
–*Publishers Weekly*

"STRONG...CLEVERLY CONSTRUCTED"
stories with an "URGENT SENSE OF
MORAL PURPOSE."
–*The New York Times Book Review*

 ST. MARTIN'S PRESS

THE MID-ATLANTIC
CREATIVE NONFICTION
SUMMER WRITERS'
CONFERENCE

BALTIMORE, MARYLAND
AUGUST 12-16, 1997

The second annual writers' conference devoted exclusively to the emerging genre of creative nonfiction, featuring distinguished guest writers and faculty.

Includes a unique "Selling What You Write" component.

For a brochure, call 1-800-697-4646 or 410-337-6200
http://www.goucher.edu/~cnf

Goucher College Center for Graduate and Continuing Studies Co-sponsored by the Creative Nonfiction Foundation

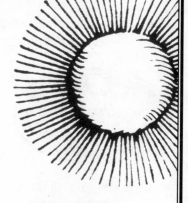

GUEST WRITERS
Tracy Kidder
Tobias Wolff
Gay Talese

CONFERENCE FACULTY
Darcy Frey
Jeanne Marie Laskas
Susan Orlean
Lauren Slater

CONFERENCE DIRECTOR
Lee Gutkind

GOUCHER COLLEGE

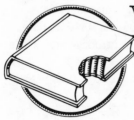

Be an Expatriate Writer for Two Weeks

Join an international group of selected fiction writers for an intensive working seminar in the tranquillity of a Dutch Renaissance castle. Guided by six distinguished instructors, this seminar is designed to be intimate and productive. The team-taught workshop is an editorial roundtable where writers are advised on strategies for analyzing structure and developing and sustaining character-in-action. Designated writing sessions and individual conferences enable new or revised work and redefined writing objectives. The seminar concentrates on the craft and technique of fiction while also considering the pragmatics of the literary market. The dynamics of the seminar are carefully planned to include both published writers and those in the early stages of promising careers. The seminar is sponsored and administered by Emerson College and inspired by the literary traditions of the journal *Ploughshares,* an Emerson College publication. Four academic credits are offered and all applications received by April 1 are considered for the $1,000 Robie Macauley fellowship.

DIRECTOR: Alexandra Marshall. FACULTY: James Carroll, Pamela Painter, Thomas E. Kennedy, Alexandra Johnson, Askold Melnyczuk.

Eighth Annual

Ploughshares International Fiction Writing Seminar

Kasteel Well
The Netherlands
August 11-22, 1997
Emerson College
European Center

For a brochure and application to the seminar, mail or fax this form to
David Griffin • Assistant Director of Continuing Education
Emerson College • 100 Beacon Street • Boston, MA 02116 USA
Tel. 617-824-8567 • Fax 617-824-8618 • E-mail: dgriffin@emerson.edu

Name _____

Address _____

_____

wc&f

MFA in Writing
at Vermont College

Intensive 11-day residencies on our beautiful central Vermont campus alternate with **six-month non-resident semester study projects**.

Residencies include classes, readings, conferences and small workshops led by two faculty. Immersed with other developing writers in a stimulating environment, students forge working relationships with each other and with experienced practitioners of poetry and fiction.

Under the careful guidance of the faculty, students focus on their own writing for the semester study project. A low student-faculty ratio (5-1) ensures close personal attention.

We also offer **Post-Graduate Semesters** and **One-Year Intensives** for those who have completed a graduate degree in creative writing.

Scholarships, minority scholarships and financial aid available.

Vermont College admits students regardless of race, creed, sex or ethnic origin.

Residencies catered by the New England Culinary Institute.

Poetry Faculty

Robin Behn
Mark Cox
Deborah Digges
Nancy Eimers
Mark Halliday
Richard Jackson
Jack Myers
William Olsen
David Rivard
J. Allyn Rosser
Mary Ruefle
Betsy Sholl
Leslie Ullman
Roger Weingarten
David Wojahn

Fiction Faculty

Carol Anshaw
Phyllis Barber
Francois Camoin
Abby Frucht
Douglas Glover
Sydney Lea
Diane Lefer
Ellen Lesser
Bret Lott
Sena Jeter Naslund
Christopher Noel
Pamela Painter
Sharon Sheehe Stark
Gladys Swan
W. D. Wetherell

For more information contact:
Roger Weingarten, Director
MFA in Writing
Vermont College
Montpelier, VT 05602
Tel: (802) 828-8840 Fax: (802) 828-8649

Vermont College of Norwich University